D1008940

One-Minute
PRAYERS®
When You
Need a Miracle

NICK HARRISON

HARVEST HOUSE PUBLISHERS
EUGENE, OREGON

Cover by Kyler Dougherty

Front cover photo © SandraMatic / Getty Images

ONE-MINUTE PRAYERS® is a registered trademark of The Hawkins
Children's LLC. Harvest House Publishers, Inc., is the exclusive licensee
of the federally registered trademark ONE-MINUTE PRAYERS.

One-Minute Prayers® When You Need a Miracle
Copyright © 2019 by Nick Harrison
Published by Harvest House Publishers
Eugene, Oregon 97408
www.harvesthousepublishers.com

ISBN 978-0-7369-7804-0 (pbk.)
ISBN 978-0-7369-7805-7 (eBook)

Library of Congress Cataloging-in-Publication Data is on file at the
Library of Congress, Washington, DC.

Printed in China
19 20 21 22 23 24 25 26 27 / RDS-GL / 9 8 7 6 5 4 3 2 1

Believer, though all things are apparently against thee, rest assured that God has made a reservation on thy behalf; in the roll of thy griefs there is a saving clause. Somehow he will deliver thee, and somewhere he will provide for thee. The quarter from which thy rescue shall arise may be a very unexpected one, but help will assuredly come in thine extremity, and thou shalt magnify the name of the Lord. If men do not feed thee, ravens shall; and if earth yield not wheat, heaven shall drop with manna. Therefore be of good courage, and rest quietly in the Lord. God can make the sun rise in the west if he pleases, and make the source of distress the channel of delight.

CHARLES HADDON SPURGEON (1834–1892)

INTRODUCTION

Are you in a desperate situation right now? Does there seem to be no way out? No escape…only an unavoidable drastic outcome to your present crisis?

In short, *you need a miracle.* You need nothing less than for God to show up and show up *big*.

It would be useless for me to offer several clichés or even Scripture verses that assure you, "God's got this. You'll be okay." That may be true, but in our darkest hours, we need more than platitudes.

My prayer is that on the following pages, you'll find hope—*real* hope—for your darkest hour. God *does* hear our prayers. There is never a moment when we and our circumstances are not on His mind. Further, God has a solution—a perfect solution—for our every situation. It's not always a solution we appreciate or anticipate, because we're not able to see our situation the way God sees it. Often, though, we can look back and see in hindsight that God had us in His hands all along.

As we walk together through the next few weeks, and as you pray the prayers in this book, I want you to learn to fully trust in God for the outcome of your situation. Trust that He sees. Trust that He knows your pain. Trust that He will come through for you.

Two things we all must keep in mind when we go through hard—even desperate—times. First, we need to know that God *does* do miracles as He answers prayers. But sometimes those miracles are not how we imagined them. God has the perfect answer for those who trust Him, but the answer or miracle doesn't always unfold the way we think it should. Can you accept that?

Second, we tend to think of miracles as always supernatural answers given right *now*. We want a *fast* miracle. And sometimes God does give us fast miracles. But sometimes God's miracles reveal themselves slowly over time. Are you willing to accept that your miracle might be a slow miracle? After all, if it's a miracle from God, whether it comes slow or fast shouldn't matter.

Here's what I want you to do as you pray the prayers in this book:

- Watch for God's answer to your prayer, realizing His miracle may not be the miracle you imagined.
- Don't let your resolve to trust Him weaken if the situation gets worse before it gets better.
- Don't keep looking at your crisis with fear, anger, or worry. Change your focus to God. Look only to Him. When Peter saw Jesus walk on water, he wanted to do so too. At Jesus's invitation, Peter got out of the boat and was doing fine as long as he kept his eyes on Jesus. But when he looked at the storm around him, he began to sink. Keep your eyes on the Lord and walk on water through your crisis.

- Thank God for the answer *now*, before it comes.
- Praise Him when it does come…and tell others of God's faithfulness to you.
- If your miracle comes before you finish this book, turn to page 171 and read "A Final Word."

Some will ask, "How can simple one-minute prayers bring about the miracle I need?" Well, all we need to do is look at many of the prayers in the Bible and notice how very short some of them are. One of the most powerful prayers in the Bible was just nine words long. The thief on the cross looked over to Jesus and simply said, "Jesus, remember me when you come into your kingdom" (Luke 23:42). That prayer was granted. There are many other short prayers throughout the Bible, including the most famous prayer of all: the Lord's Prayer. Martin Luther is quoted as saying, "The fewer the words, the better the prayer." Brevity is not our enemy when we pray. But long prayers are welcome to God too. My hope is that if you find a minute too short a time to pray, you will use these prayers as a jump start to your own longer prayers. If that happens, good! *Keep praying.* One minute is the minimum, not the maximum. Pray as long as you need to, even if you have to ask God to give you the words to keep praying. One advantage of a crisis is that it teaches us to pray!

Some readers will be tempted to skip ahead and read more than one prayer. I suggest you resist that temptation and read just one prayer a day, allowing yourself to reflect on it until the next day. Consider its message. Make its truth your truth before you move on. One reason not to skip ahead is that several themes are repeated throughout the book. These are important and need to be said again in a slightly different way. These themes include faith, patience, trust, and God's sovereignty. It's important that you internalize these spiritual truths through repetition.

Finally, please remember that this book is based on a Christian understanding of God and how He works, as revealed in the Bible. Know that the greatest miracle of all happens when we are born again into the kingdom of God by asking Christ to take charge of our life. That is the first miracle you must start with. Trust Him with your life—this life and eternal life. If you have never received Christ as your Lord, I suggest you do so now and begin to live out the greatest miracle of all. Here's a suggested prayer:

> God, I need Your help. I need *You* in my life. I ask You to forgive my sins and create in me the new, abundant life You promise those who believe in You. God, I commit my present situation and my entire self to You. Thank You for loving me and hearing my prayer.

If you prayed that prayer and meant it, God heard it and, according to His Word, you are now His child.

If you're already a Christian, my hope is that this book will help you stretch your faith and enlarge your view of God.

Now, let's get to praying for your miracle!

THE FULLNESS OF TIME

When the fullness of the time had come...
GALATIANS 4:4 NKJV

When we're in deep trouble, we want a solution *now*. Our need for a miracle won't wait. And yet, God is the Lord of time. He knows when and how to answer our prayer. There's no sense in rushing God's answer. It's enough to know He *is* going to answer...in the fullness of time.

In the meantime, persist in prayer.

Heavenly Father, I'm not good at waiting, especially during this hard time I'm going through. You know the depth of my situation. You know how much I want a miracle *now*. Help me as I learn to wait. Help me accept *Your* time for the miracle I need. Forgive me for my impatience. Remind me of Your faithfulness to me in the past so that I trust You fully for the future. Lord, I know You already see the outcome of my situation. You're not worried or stressed. For that reason, I, too, will rest and wait until the fullness of time has come.

Trust

When I am afraid,
I put my trust in you.
In God, whose word I praise,
in God I trust; I shall not be afraid.

Psalm 56:3-4

God allows certain adverse situations in our life as a chance for us to exercise our trust in Him. We ask ourselves, *Will God come through for me again?* Then we look back and see His hand in our previous hard situations and know that, yes, He is worthy to be trusted...even in *this*.

Dear Lord, You have given me so many opportunities to trust You. I've not always been good at it, but time after time, You've come through for me even when my trust was weak. I pray now for a trusting heart in my present situation. I pray that the end of my trial will find me more trusting of You and more aware of the power of trust to help me overcome the problems I face in the future. With the psalmist, I know that my fears will diminish as I trust in You. No, I shall not be afraid.

GOD WILL GET THE GLORY

To him be glory forever. Amen.
ROMANS 11:36

It's so important that, as early as possible in our dilemma, we come to the end of ourselves. We need to commit the cause of our turmoil to God with the full understanding that He alone will receive the glory when a miracle presents itself. If truth be told, many of us forget this important principle. Our issue becomes resolved, and we may give a nod to God for His part while not fully giving Him all the praise, glory, and honor for what He's done. Make sure now, not later, that you ascribe to God the praise due Him for His intervention.

O God, how foolish it would be for me to take any glory from the miracle to come. Or to give praise to others when I know full well *You* have brought about the miracle I've waited for. Even now, before the resolution comes, I give You the advance praise and glory for what You're doing behind the scenes and what You will do in the future to secure the right outcome for my situation. Yes, Lord, to You alone belongs all the praise and thanksgiving. Truly, You are a God of miracles and wonders.

FEELING ALONE

*Father of the fatherless and protector of widows
is God in his holy habitation.
God settles the solitary in a home;
he leads out the prisoners to prosperity,
but the rebellious dwell in a parched land.*

PSALM 68:5-6

When we're in a desperate situation, we feel alone. Even though we know intellectually that others have gone through tough times before us—and *are* going through tough times now, and *will* go through tough times in the future—it doesn't make our struggle any easier. We still feel like no one can possibly understand. But God does understand. Know this: *We are never alone in our trials.*

Dear Lord, my situation is hard to bear today. I feel like no one understands, even as they express their sympathy and offer their prayers. Please God, father of the fatherless and protector of widows, refresh my spirit by giving me a sense of Your presence. May I carry that sense through the days ahead as I watch You move toward a resolution in my situation. Lord, replace the loneliness with the comfort only You can provide. Lead me out of my desert into a place of peaceful prosperity.

CONFIDENCE IN GOD'S WORK

In the fear of the Lord one has strong confidence.
PROVERBS 14:26

Seeing God work builds our confidence. We move from victory to victory in life as time after time He proves Himself faithful. Have confidence today in God's ability to work out every issue in your life. After all, He's shown you countless times that you can always turn to Him, no matter the obstacle you face.

God, my confidence in You is strong. I'm convinced You can do what needs to be done to get me through this rough patch. It will take a miracle, but I'm confident that You can provide one, Lord. You are the author of miracles, and I believe You have one waiting with my name on it.

And, Father, when this time of trial is over, I will look back and see the miracle as a trophy of Your faithfulness and yet another confirmation of my confidence in You.

You are ever loyal to me, Lord.

EXPECTING A MIRACLE

With God all things are possible.
MATTHEW 19:26

To *receive* a miracle, we must *expect* a miracle. We must believe that God does the impossible. We must know that He is here with us in our trial and has a desired end in mind. We must never allow doubts to undermine our expectation.

God, You are Lord of the impossible. You know I need You to do what seems to me to be impossible. Father, my expectation for a miracle is from You and You alone. Bear with me as I build my confidence in Your ability to bring this crisis to your desired end. Bring good fruit from what now seems like a lost cause.

Father, with You all things are possible.

BE OPEN TO A SURPRISE ANSWER

*He ordered the crowds to sit down on the grass,
and taking the five loaves and the two fish, he
looked up to heaven and said a blessing. Then he
broke the loaves and gave them to the disciples,
and the disciples gave them to the crowds.*

MATTHEW 14:19

In the chaos of our situation, we may have reasoned out the exact miracle God should give us. But God, in giving us our miracle, may surprise us with an answer we hadn't expected. We must be open to His surprising miracle, setting aside our own—usually faulty—designs for an outcome.

God, You are unpredictable! So unpredictable that You can feed more than five thousand people with five loaves and two fish—and have twelve baskets of leftovers. What a miraculous answer to a very real need.

Lord, I love Your unpredictability, even though it often confuses me. Please know that I want *Your* miracle for my chaotic situation. I accept that it may not be the one I have in mind. I accept that Your miracle will result in a better end than "mine."

Lord, surprise me. Delight me with Your answer.

Dependency on God

Trust in the Lord with all your heart,
and do not lean on your own understanding.

PROVERBS 3:5

Turbulence in our life forces us to relinquish control and utterly trust God with all our heart. We can no longer lean on our own understanding. Perhaps this is the reason God is allowing our current trial—to ensure that we trust fully in Him and abandon our own faulty understanding. Don't miss the lesson God has for you as He reinforces your need to depend on Him and Him alone.

Father, this situation has knocked all the props out from under me. I have no crutches to lean on. My own understanding will not bring about a solution. I have only You, so I cast myself anew on You for Your strength, for the courage You can give, for the peace of Your Holy Spirit amid my present turmoil.

Lord, I ask You to allow this trial to increase my dependence on You in every area of my life.

LAMENT

Their heart cried to the Lord.
O wall of the daughter of Zion,
let tears stream down like a torrent day and night!
Give yourself no rest, your eyes no respite!...
Pour out your heart like water
before the presence of the Lord!
LAMENTATIONS 2:18-19

Lamenting is a fully biblical concept. In fact, one book of the Bible is even called "Lamentations." God's people have often had to lament the adverse circumstances happening to them. God does not begrudge us our time of grieving during a crisis. Today, if your heart is heavy due to your present ordeal, go ahead and mourn. Pour out your heart to God. He listens intently to our lamentations.

God, You know my concerns. You know my pain. You hear my cries...my lamentations. Today, I can barely pray for my need; I can only lament, knowing You understand. I submit my pain, confusion, frustration, and even anger to You. It's just so hard to believe this will turn out all right.

Hear my cry, Lord! Listen to my prayers!
Send help to me, Father! I so desperately need it.

THE GOD-DIRECTED LIFE

Many are the afflictions of the righteous,
but the LORD delivers him out of them all.

PSALM 34:19

True happiness comes from a life fully surrendered to God. This surrender results in a "God-directed life." It means that God brings focus, direction, and good into our days. However, we still endure trials. Sometimes severe trials. Yes, "many are the afflictions of the righteous." But the God-directed person knows that God delivers His people from their adversity and uses those trials for the ultimate benefit of the person going through them.

Are you being directed by God? Is He at the center of your life? If so, allow Him to lead you to your trials and through your trials. He will bring about the God-directed miracle.

Father, as best I know how to do, I offer my life up as a God-directed life. Help me trust You through everything—the good, the bad, and the ugly. When I face a severe adversity, such as the one I'm enduring now, I know You can turn the trial into a God-directed opportunity for my benefit—even if that benefit is simply using my experience to help others as they go through the same adversity.

Lord, I surrender my life to You and ask You to direct me through this and every adversity.

Acknowledging the Pain

You have kept count of my tossings;
put my tears in your bottle
Are they not in your book?

PSALM 56:8

God is okay with us acknowledging our pain as we go through our trial. We can, in fact, confidently cry out to Him through each pang of sorrow or confusion. Even Jesus on the cross cried out to His Father. So, let God hear your sobs. Let Him place your tears in His bottle. You are not forgotten. He, too, acknowledges your pain.

O God! My heart is heavy as I move through this stage of my life. I look back and wonder how...why...when will it end? Dear Father, I cry out to You with tears borne from my pain. Hear the cry of my heart. Bear this pain with me, Lord. Take note of my tears; put them in Your bottle. Let not one tear fall unseen by You. Endure the pain with me, Father. And when the time for crying is past, may I reap the joy that comes with the morning.

To keep our hand on the plow while wiping
away our tears—that is Christianity!

WATCHMAN NEE (1903–1972)

GOD CHANGES WHAT
YOU CANNOT

*Ah, Lord GOD! It is you who have made the heavens
and the earth by your great power and by your
outstretched arm! Nothing is too hard for you.*
JEREMIAH 32:17

Most of our severest trials leave us powerless to change the circumstances or bring the situation to a close. We cannot wave a wand and have our ordeal end simply because we wish it so. When that truth finally sinks in—that our only recourse is to trust God—we should feel a sense of relief. We are powerless, but He is all-powerful. He can change what we cannot.

Father, You see how helpless I am in my current situation. There is nothing I know to do to bring about the needed miracle. Lord, I must trust in You, the God who has made heaven and earth by His great power and outstretched arm.

Please intervene on my behalf by that same power and outstretched arm. Lord, devise and bring to pass the very miracle needed to end this terrible situation. Do for me what I cannot do for myself. Thank You for Your divine intervention in my situation.

In Quietness and Confidence

Thus says the Lord GOD, the Holy One of Israel:
"In returning and rest you shall be saved;
in quietness and confidence shall be your strength."

ISAIAH 30:15 NKJV

So often our troubling situations cause us to become emotionally distraught or propel us into needless worry. We are anything but quiet and confident. And yet, when we trust in God for our miracle, we find a quietness and confidence that settle us as we prayerfully wait for His movement in our ordeal.

Rest easy today—as best you can. Be quiet before the Lord. Be confident.

O Lord, how hard it is to remain quiet and on an even keel emotionally while all this is going on. Still my soul, Father. Bring to my emotions the peace that comes from trusting in You. When I'm tempted to move out of my quiet and confident zone, rein me in. Keep me within the protective circle of Your love and care.

SHARING YOUR BURDEN

Bear one another's burdens, and so fulfill the law of Christ.
GALATIANS 6:2

Bearing a heavy burden alone makes the load even more crushing. Do you have others with whom you can share your need for a miracle? Can you call on two or three people with whom you can share the intimate details of your situation? Enlist at least two prayer partners and bring them into your circle of pain. Ask them to remember you when they pray. Update them weekly or even daily if necessary with additional needs that may arise due to your situation. These prayer partners can share your burden. And then as the miracle comes to pass, they can also rejoice with you.

Father God, lead me to two or three others whom I can trust with my burden. Bring to mind the ones You would have me enlist in the fight. Help me become transparent about my need. Increase their sensitivity toward me. As they pray for me, may they also become my encouragers during the heat of battle. Then, Father, as my trial draws to a close, always remind me how much I needed and appreciated others who were willing to walk with me. Enlist me, dear Lord, in then becoming a sharer of others' burdens.

KNOWING GOD CARES

O God, do not keep silence;
do not hold your peace or be still, O God!
PSALM 83:1

As we wait for a miracle, sometimes God seems silent in response to our prayers, oblivious to our tears. And yet, we must know of a certainty that God is ever at work on our behalf, even during the silent hours, days, or weeks. Keep trusting day by day in the God who cares.

God, I don't much like it when You're silent. I want to feel Your presence throughout my trial. I want to hear Your words of comfort. I want to see You move on my behalf.

On those days when I feel particularly alone and cannot sense Your presence, remind me that You're never far away. You are here, even though I can't hear Your voice. On those days when my prayers seem to stop at the ceiling, remind me that You are still aware of my desperate need.

OVERCOMING DOUBT

The mountains melt like wax before the LORD,
before the Lord of all the earth.
PSALM 97:5

At some point in our desert journey, we may face a huge dune of doubt. We wonder, *Can I possibly keep going? Must I trudge up this mountain of sand, my feet slipping backward with each step forward?* This dune of doubt may be built up slowly, a trickle each day, or it may rush upon us like a brisk sandstorm, planting the dune in front of us, where before we saw nothing but an even path. No matter how it comes, the mountain must be climbed. We must make our way onward—trusting, praying, even rejoicing as we go on our way. We can do this. With each step, we can watch the mountain melt like wax before the Lord.

O God, the mountain of doubt seems to appear just when I least need it. It assaults my faith with what-ifs and if-onlys and the thought, "There is no hope for you." Lord, be with me as I traverse the mountain. Give me wings of faith to fly over the dry and dusty dune of doubt.

Father, bring me back to faith—full faith—quickly. Remove every future mountain that would attempt to discourage me afresh. Melt it like wax.

Tactics of the Enemy

We would not be outwitted by Satan; for
we are not ignorant of his designs.

2 Corinthians 2:11

If we look behind every monumental trial we face, we can see the design of the enemy to bring us down, one way or the other. If the trial itself won't destroy us, perhaps the stress will do it. That's the downside of our situation.

Conversely, we know that God is *for* us, no matter how Satan attempts to bring us down. We see this in the life of Job. We see it in the Old Testament story of Joseph, whose brothers meant to do him harm. In the end, Joseph could say, "You meant evil against me, but God meant it for good" (Genesis 50:20). We even see it in Jesus. With Jesus hanging on the cross, the enemy thought he had won; but in reality, the crucifixion was his undoing.

Know the tactics of the enemy as you walk through your trial. Never let him have the upper hand. Stay strong in God!

Dear Lord, I can see the hand of Satan in my situation. He means to wreak havoc in my life through doubt and discouragement. God, I pray for Your protection as I move ahead day by day. I pray, too, for

Your sovereign power to bring the ultimate good out of this. Even if I never live to understand that good, I trust You will still bring it to pass. Redeem my situation, God. Bring about the miracle I need.

The Role of Worship

Ascribe to the LORD the glory due his name;
worship the LORD in the splendor of holiness.

PSALM 29:2

In prayer, we're engaging in thanksgiving and intercession for ourselves (and others), and we're listening to God speak. Worship is often a part of prayer—though we can pray and not truly worship, and we can worship and not truly pray.

In the midst of your trial, take time not merely to pray, but to worship God. Worship Him not for what He can do (though that's important), but *for who He is*. Quietly bow before Him and offer words of praise. Adore Him. Worship your king in all His majesty. Glory in your God today. Revel in worshipping Him.

Lord God, You are so beautiful. You are worthy of all my worship and praise, not for what You can do for me, but for who You are. I ascribe to You praise and adoration. I sing the glory of Your name. You are Lord of my life, owner of my heart, lover of my soul, author and finisher of my faith.

Yes, God to You be all the praise...all the worship... all the glory.

KNOWING ALL WILL BE WELL

Fear not, for I am with you;
be not dismayed, for I am your God;
I will strengthen you, I will help you,
I will uphold you with my righteous right hand.

ISAIAH 41:10

Have you realized yet that everything is going to be okay...eventually? There's no place in the Bible where we read that God utterly abandoned His people, nor does He refuse to listen to the prayers of those who come before Him in faith. Whatever your desperate situation, it *is* going to turn out well in the end, according to His will.

Keep praying, keep hoping, keep trusting. Come soon to that place of knowing all will be well at the end of your journey and you will find peace of mind.

Father, You are my sovereign God. You uphold me with Your righteous right hand. You are my God, and I will not be dismayed. My situation is ever before You. You see the beginning and the end. You know my urgent need, and You hear my prayer for a miracle.

God, I walk by faith—and certainly not by sight—as I make my way along these dangerous cliffs like a blind person. Remind me often, Lord, that this situation has an end. Through a miracle of Your making, You will bring about the right resolution according to Your will. Lord, bring it to pass!

When the trial comes upon you, what a help it would be for you if you could view it thus, "This trial is sent for my good. It does not spring out of the dust. The Lord Himself is the supreme disposer of it. It is very painful to bear; but let me believe that He has appointed me this peculiar trial, along with every other circumstance. He will bring about His own will therein, and either remove the trial, or give me patience under it, and submission to it."

J.C. Philpot (1802–1869)

Rejoicing in the Lord

Rejoice in the Lord always; again I will say, rejoice.
PHILIPPIANS 4:4

In God's pharmacy, there are several proven remedies for just about every malady. When we're weak from our arduous journey, one of the best remedies is the joy of the Lord. Usually when we're tired, we're fully depleted of our joy. *Our* joy is always capable of vanishing when trouble hits. However, the *Lord's* joy—the joy that He brings to our heart—is endless, tireless. Paul could easily tell the Philippian Christians to "rejoice…and again I say rejoice!" Rejoice just now in the joy of the Lord. Drink in deeply.

Lord, thank You for the joy You bring! Your joy is like a living spring, gushing with refreshing water in a dry land.

More, Lord, more! Pour out Your joy on me as I rejoice in You. Bring the optimism and hopefulness to my soul that is born of true joy. God, I do not rejoice in myself and certainly not in my circumstances. No, I rejoice only in You. Praise You for the joyful heart You bring me, Lord!

COMMITTED

Commit your way to the LORD;
trust in him, and he will act.

PSALM 37:5

Once we commit our life to the Lord, our circumstances—including future events—come along with it. Perhaps we could not have foreseen our present trial, but it is now part of our life. God accepts, as part of our commitment to Him, the present situation. In short, our trial is also *His* trial. All that we commit to Him becomes His as well as ours.

God, you know all I have is Yours. All I *am* is Yours. When I commit to You, I commit *all* to You. I commit to You this trial with all its troubling tentacles. Lord, take what I have and make it Yours. Take this trial and turn it inside out to serve Your purposes. It is no longer mine alone. And Lord, in a similar way, all You have is mine. I take, then, Your peace as mine. Your joy too.

THE FUTURE IS A ROAD

I know the plans I have for you, declares the LORD,
plans for welfare and not for evil,
to give you a future and a hope.
JEREMIAH 29:11

When we're knee-deep in the weeds of our dilemma, our vision of the future is distorted. We see only as far down the road as our trial allows us. It becomes hard to envision a positive future wherein God has resolved our desperate situation. But difficult or not, we need to allow God to bring about hope of a future when our present trial becomes a past marker of God's faithfulness. Keep looking ahead…beyond the trial. God is there.

Father, my vision seems to be so taken up with my troubles, I can't see the days ahead as anything but more struggle. Help me fix my eyes on a future when my present trial has become a memorial to Your faithfulness to me. Encourage me, Lord, to look ahead into the destiny You've prepared for me. Help me as I lay aside the difficulties that have led to my present crisis. May they pass as quickly as You will allow.

THE HOLY SPIRIT AS COMFORTER

Blessed be the God and Father of our Lord Jesus Christ,
the Father of mercies and God of all comfort, who
comforts us in all our affliction, so that we may be able
to comfort those who are in any affliction, with the
comfort with which we ourselves are comforted by God.

2 CORINTHIANS 1:3-4

The Holy Spirit has many roles in our life—teacher, guide, helper, and much more. But in our present situation, perhaps the most meaningful role is that of comforter. During our every pang of pain, the Holy Spirit is there to comfort. We receive this comfort just like everything else in the Christian life—by faith. Do not go one more day without the comfort of the Holy Spirit. Then resolve to comfort others in their affliction with the same comfort you have received from God.

Holy Spirit, thank You for Your presence in my life. Thank You for leading me, guiding me, teaching me. Thank You for revealing to me the Lord Jesus Christ and His power to save me. Now in my time of trial, I thank You most for being my comforter. I pray for a distinct sense of Your holy presence during each step I take. Thank You, Lord, for becoming as a pillow under my head during this time of upheaval.

Clear Thinking

God has not given us a spirit of fear, but of power and of love and of a sound mind.

2 Timothy 1:7 nkjv

Are we thinking clearly when we go through the furnace of affliction? Not always. Our mind is so occupied with our troubles that we often no longer think objectively. Here's an example: If we have, say, an adult child on drugs, we may think that harboring and aiding him or her is compassion, when it's really enablement. Or if we're in a physically abusive relationship, we may excuse the abuse or find reasons why we should accept it as inevitable.

Think about your present trial. Ask yourself how it may be affecting your ability to think clearly. Ask God to help you view your situation the way He sees it.

Father God, help me see and think clearly as I move through this time of affliction. Remove the blinders that cause me to make excuses for my behavior or the behavior of others. Show me how You see my situation. Show me the *truth* of the matter. Encourage me to make decisions based on Your Word and the leading of Your Holy Spirit. Help me set aside any unclear thinking. Give me the fruit that comes from having a sound mind.

Thank You, Lord, for helping me think rightly and thus act rightly.

THAT THE WORKS OF GOD MAY BE DISPLAYED

*As [Jesus] passed by, he saw a man blind from birth. And
his disciples asked him, "Rabbi, who sinned, this man
or his parents, that he was born blind?" Jesus answered,
"It was not that this man sinned, or his parents, but
that the works of God might be displayed in him."*

JOHN 9:1-3

When we try to figure out "Why me, Lord?" we're
often at a loss. We simply don't know why we're
undergoing this severe trial. In such cases, let's refer back
to the man who had been born blind, but was healed by
Jesus. When asked what had caused his blindness, Jesus
replied that the reason was so the works of God could
be displayed by the man's healing.

No matter what the genesis of our trouble, let's
attribute the origin—and the outcome—to a display
of God's work.

Father, I don't know why I'm going through this horrible trial. I've tried to figure it out, and yet I remain clueless. Lord, may the reason for all this chaos be that You end up being glorified in some way. Take this situation and turn it into a monument to Your faithfulness. May others see Your kindness to me and glorify Your name—as I do, Lord.

God's Love for You

*See what kind of love the Father has given to us, that
we should be called children of God; and so we are.*

1 John 3:1

In the midst of our troubles, it's possible to lose sight of God's overwhelming love for us. But it's during the time of trouble that we most need to be assured of God's love. No matter how you feel about the direction your life has taken, you can still daily live in the love of God.

Lord, there is healing in Your love for me, one of Your children. Help me today to experience that love...to sense it in a real way. Help me learn to live daily in Your love. Remind me of the many ways You care for me. Never let me abandon hope through discouragement. Rather, renew my confidence that Your love will pave the way to my miracle.

FORGIVENESS

Be kind to one another, tenderhearted, forgiving
one another, as God in Christ forgave you.
EPHESIANS 4:32

For some of us, our troubles may contain an aspect of offense. Or perhaps, the result of our troubles may cause offense. In either case, forgiveness is an important element in our healing.

Look at your situation carefully. Is there someone you need to forgive? Is there someone who needs to forgive you? Opening the door to forgiveness may bring about the very miracle you're waiting for.

God, I thank You for forgiving me in Christ. Thank You that You no longer count my offenses against me. Lord, if there's any element of forgiveness needed to hasten the miracle in my present situation, please make me aware of it. Help me become an easy forgiver toward those who have wronged me. May others have no cause to forgive me for bringing offense to them, but if they do, make that plain, too, Father. I want no offense to stand between me and the miracle that will resolve my trial.

GOD'S FAVOR

You bless the righteous, O LORD;
you cover him with favor as with a shield.
PSALM 5:12

It's not wrong to ask God to bring favor into your situation. In fact, it's necessary and right to do so. Let God's favor for you recast how you look at your present circumstances. Let His favor be a shield against trouble.

God, it amazes me that You've chosen to favor me. I don't deserve such treatment, and yet I welcome it. Father, may Your favor extend to my present situation. May it influence others in my circle so as to bring about healing and peace. Lord, may I in turn influence others to trust in Your generous favor. Let it be a shield covering me, hiding me from trouble.

He who dwells in the shelter of the Most High
will abide in the shadow of the Almighty.
I will say to the LORD, "My refuge and my fortress,
my God, in whom I trust."

For he will deliver you from the snare of the fowler
and from the deadly pestilence.
He will cover you with his pinions,
and under his wings you will find refuge;
his faithfulness is a shield and buckler.

You will not fear the terror of the night,
nor the arrow that flies by day,
nor the pestilence that stalks in darkness,
nor the destruction that wastes at noonday.

A thousand may fall at your side,
ten thousand at your right hand,
but it will not come near you.
PSALM 91:1-7

A PLEA FOR SAFETY

A thousand may fall at your side,
ten thousand at your right hand,
but it will not come near you.

PSALM 91:7

Is there an element of danger in your situation? Make part of your prayers a plea for safety. May a thousand fall on your right and on your left, but may it not come near you. May you not fear the terror of the night nor the arrow that flies by day (verse 5). May your life be surrounded by divine safety.

God, during this stressful time, watch over me. Protect me from danger. Extend, Lord, Your safety net over my loved ones. Bring any plans of harm toward me to naught. Increase my faith to resist unreasonable fears brought on by tempting thoughts to doubt Your protection. Guard me, Lord. Send angels to encamp around me. Stave off every danger.

GOD'S UNIQUE PLAN FOR YOU

When you go through deep waters, I will be with you.
When you go through rivers of difficulty,
you will not drown.
When you walk through the fire of oppression,
you will not be burned up;
the flames will not consume you.
For I am the LORD, your God,
the Holy One of Israel, your Savior.

ISAIAH 43:2-3 NLT

God has a unique plan for each of us. Sometimes accomplishing that plan requires us to go through deep waters. During that time, all we see is the murky, churning sea. God sees the end, though, and when we're committed to Him and His plan, we can be assured of a safe ending to our journey.

God, I'm in the deep waters of life now. If this is part of Your plan for me, I pray that the work will quickly be accomplished so I can move on, past this pain. Bring whatever good you desire from my situation and help me recognize the part this agony plays in Your plan for my life.

Bring good fruit from this desperate situation.

HE WILL NOT LEAVE OR
FORSAKE YOU—EVER

Be strong and courageous. Do not fear or be in
dread of them, for it is the LORD your God who goes
with you. He will not leave you or forsake you.

DEUTERONOMY 31:6

As we wait, watch, and pray for our miracle, it's comforting to know that our Lord is always with us. There isn't a solitary second that He's not only present, but also active on our behalf. We don't always sense His presence, but the promise is sure: He is here. We are not forsaken.

Dear Lord, days go by, and I don't sense Your presence. By faith, I know that even during those times, You're here with me. I'm not going through this trial alone. Your promises are "as good as gold," and right now I'm relying on Your assurance that You're with me *always*. You see the end from the beginning, and You have already determined how to work out my situation in the best way possible. I trust You, Lord. Thank You for Your presence, whether I feel it or not.

Father, because of Your presence, I am strong and courageous. I do not fear, nor am I in dread of my circumstances, for You have gone before me. Praise You, Lord!

GOD IS A PROMISE KEEPER

All the promises of God find their Yes in [Jesus].
2 CORINTHIANS 1:20

One of the worst accusations Satan whispers in our ear is that God will not keep His promises. Such an idea is unthinkable for the trusting Christian. Time after time, God has shown Himself to be true to His Word. And yet, when we're going through a rough patch, we become vulnerable to Satan's lies. At such times, we need to find a relevant promise in God's Word and stand firm on it, reminding Satan of God's solid commitment to us. Silence him with the promises of God.

God, like any great father, You are always true to me. You keep Your promises, despite the treasonous whispers of the enemy. Lord, I find my strength for the fight in Your Word. When doubt assails me, direct me to the exact promise from Your Word that will empower me to stand strong. Through Your promises, may I silence the enemy's accusations and fearmongering.

Lord, I revel in Your faithful promises!

ABIDING IN THE VINE

*Abide in me, and I in you. As the branch cannot
bear fruit by itself, unless it abides in the vine,
neither can you, unless you abide in me. I am
the vine; you are the branches. Whoever abides
in me and I in him, he it is that bears much
fruit, for apart from me you can do nothing.*
JOHN 15:4-5

Where is the safest place for the believer to abide? In the vine, of course—and Jesus is the vine. When we abide in Him, we have true life. If we will not abide in Him, we suffer great loss.

Lord, I abide in You, my true vine. Supply me with all I need to get through my present ordeal. Refresh me with Your divine life. Flow through me and allow me to bear Your presence when I'm with others who struggle. May my abiding life become a testimony to Your faithfulness. May the fruit of the vine be peace, love, and joy in my life through the Holy Spirit.

The Power to Make a Decision

I will instruct you and teach you in the way you should go;
I will counsel you with my eye upon you.

PSALM 32:8

One of our greatest freedoms in Christ is the power to make right decisions. Perhaps our present situation requires us to make such a choice. We are at a fork in the road. This way or that way? God gives wisdom as we decide in faith, but then we must put that decision to work on our behalf. Don't be wishy-washy. Prayerfully decide and then, in faith, follow through on that wise decision.

Father, sometimes I make halfhearted decisions. It almost feels like flipping a coin. But God, You are full of wisdom that You're willing to impart to me. So Lord, I ask now for Your wisdom. Guide me as I make my small and large decisions.

Regarding my present situation, I pray for the courage to make the necessary decisions and follow through on them. As I do, I trust You to step in and turn those wise decisions into the roadway for the miracle I need.

Your View of God
Is Too Small

Great is our Lord, and abundant in power;
his understanding is beyond measure.

PSALM 147:5

When doubts inevitably arise, it's often because we've allowed our view of God to become too small, too limited in imagining what He can or can't do. At such times, we need to step back and regain our sense of God as omnipotent, omniscient, and omnipresent. God is never small, never limited, and does not know the word "impossible." Make sure you're trusting in the true God, not the small, ineffectual god that exists nowhere but in the lies of Satan. Be bold in your belief in our mighty God!

God, I worship You as the great creator and sustainer of the universe. You are greatly to be praised. I marvel at Your abundant power. Your understanding is beyond measure. Lord, it is because of Your greatness that I trust You for the perfect, miraculous resolution to the issue plaguing me now. I hold fast to the knowledge that *nothing is impossible* with You. I can have faith in You, the powerful God who moves mountains in response to prayer.

PLEAD YOUR CASE

He answered, "It is not right to take the children's bread and throw it to the dogs." She said, "Yes, Lord, yet even the dogs eat the crumbs that fall from their masters' table." Then Jesus answered her, "O woman, great is your faith! Be it done for you as you desire." And her daughter was healed instantly.

MATTHEW 15:26-28

Our God is a God who listens to us as we plead our case. As you pray for your miracle, lay it all out before Him, including reasons why He should move on your behalf. In the story above, a Canaanite woman was making a ruckus with her pleas for Jesus to heal her daughter. Jesus responded, "I was sent only to the lost sheep of the house of Israel" (verse 24). That didn't stop this persistent woman. She came back reasoning that even the dogs get the crumbs from their masters' table. That faithful woman received her miracle.

There are other places in the Bible where God commends those who persistently reason with Him in prayer. Convince God of your need by pouring out your heart, offering reasons why you long for God to intervene.

Lord, like the Canaanite woman who would not be deterred, so, too, I present my case for why you should attend to my pleas. Here then, Father, are reasons why I believe you, my faithful God, should send the remedy for my situation: [Briefly give the Lord three or more reasons why you believe He should intervene in your situation].

The Power of God's Word

All Scripture is breathed out by God and profitable for teaching, for reproof, for correction, and for training in righteousness, that the man of God may be complete, equipped for every good work.

2 Timothy 3:16-17

God has given us His Word, the Bible, as a revelation of who He is. It's a book full of promises, assurances, and comfort for every possible circumstance in life. Truth be told, God's Word has power to change us and our circumstances. During our hard times, it's imperative we know and rely on it. It becomes a refuge for us, a lamp for our feet. Take every opportunity during this season to pore over Scripture, discover new promises, and find fresh hope. Delight yourself in God's Word.

O God, thank You for Your Word! Thank You for the promises, principles, and power of the Bible. Lord, use this time in my life to strengthen my knowledge of Your Word. Refresh me with a new understanding of how my life is supposed to work when guided by Your principles. Help me as I use the "sword of the Spirit" against the enemy and his tactics to bring me down. Lord, most of all, give me a fresh and unrelenting hunger for Your Word.

Your Emotions

Casting all your anxieties on him, because he cares for you.
1 Peter 5:7

During our sojourn through the valley, we often let our emotions get the best of us. We feel sad, discouraged, hopeless, confused, annoyed, or angry. Sometimes it's a mixture of all these roiling emotions. But from God's point of view, nothing has changed. The resolution to our problem—the end of the valley—is in God's sight. We are still safe under His protective eye.

When the emotions surge, simmer them down through prayer and a confession of God's promises. In other words, insist that the subjective (your emotions) be under the dominion of the objective (God's promise to resolve your hard situation).

Lord, there go my emotions again. I hear a bad report, or I assume the worst about the turn of events, and off I go on an out-of-control roller-coaster ride of subjective feelings. And yet, all during my emotional upheaval, nothing has changed from Your point of view. You are not dismayed, confused, or worried about the outcome. My trust in You has assured me that, in the end, all will be well. *And if all is not well, then it is not the end.*

LET THE LORD HELP
YOUR UNBELIEF

*The father of the child cried out and
said, "I believe; help my unbelief!"*

MARK 9:24

Who could not have sympathy for the father who brought his mute, convulsing son to Jesus to be healed? When Jesus admonished the man to have faith, he cried out, "I believe; help my unbelief!" My copy of the Bible has a footnote indicating that some manuscripts say his cry was accompanied by tears. We can well believe that. This man needed a miracle. But his faith was accompanied by a measure of unbelief.

When we're in need of God's intervention, we all are a little like that man. We do believe, but this is such a desperate situation, and we harbor a measure of unbelief. Jesus understood the father's desperation and healed his son. It's okay for you to cry out in like manner, "Lord, I believe; help my unbelief!"

Father, I see Your hand at work in my life, both in the past and in the present. This current trial is a hard one, and though I do believe, Lord, I still harbor a measure of unbelief. I pray You will look at my belief and intervene for me, despite my lingering doubts.

Have mercy on me, Father, and forgive my unbelief. Bolster my faith in You. Show Your strong hand in bringing a remedy—a miracle—to my desperate situation. I will give You the praise forever. I will not forget.

DIVINE REST

Come to me, all who labor and are heavy laden,
and I will give you rest. Take my yoke upon you,
and learn from me, for I am gentle and lowly in
heart, and you will find rest for your souls. For
my yoke is easy, and my burden is light.
MATTHEW 11:28-30

Our situation brings struggle. We are not at rest internally. We are "heavy laden." And yet, God can bring us rest if we will trust Him. He can still our turmoil if we're confident that He is in charge of the outcome of our trial.

We must take upon ourselves His gentle yoke. Our own heaviness must come off. We must remove it ourselves, by faith, and put on—with great joy—the yoke that brings rest to our souls. The yoke that is easy. The burden that is light.

Father, I come to You as one who is "heavy laden." I take off my burdensome yoke and put on Your gentle and easy yoke instead. I wear it as one wears a life jacket. For Your yoke is my place of rest. It's my refuge for the duration of the storm. I wear it with joy as I await Your miracle—Your resolution to my hard trial. As I take on Your light burden, I ask You to assume responsibility for my heavy load.

Incremental Miracles

*Some people brought to him a blind man and begged him
to touch him. And he took the blind man by the hand
and led him out of the village, and when he had spit on
his eyes and laid his hands on him, he asked him, "Do
you see anything?" And he looked up and said, "I see
people, but they look like trees, walking." Then Jesus
laid his hands on his eyes again; and he opened his eyes,
his sight was restored, and he saw everything clearly.*

MARK 8:22-25

When we think of miracles in the Bible, we often
think of the instant healings Jesus did during
His ministry. But some miracles are incremental. God
takes His time. Sometimes His work is done in stages,
like with the blind man who, at Jesus's first touch, could
only see men as trees walking. It took a second touch
for him to see perfectly. Can you accept an incremental
miracle, if that's what God chooses to give you?

Dear Lord, sometimes You do things very rapidly.
Other times, it seems like You take Your time exercis-
ing Your will. In my case, I've prayed for a miracle and
would love to see it happen as quickly as possible. But
Lord, You know best. If my miracle must unfold over
the course of days, weeks, months, or even years, so
be it. I will bow to Your perfect timing in bringing about
my miracle.

ENDURING HARD TIMES

We rejoice in our sufferings, knowing that suffering
produces endurance, and endurance produces
character, and character produces hope.
ROMANS 5:3-4

Hard times reveal what we're made of. Can we withstand stress? Is our present situation going to bring us down...or make us stronger? Truth be told, there is a measure of stress that could bring any person down. We all have a breaking point. But if we learn quickly that huge burdens—our trials, our troubles—are designed not only to reveal what we're made of, but to cause us to enter into a divine strength that far surpasses our own natural strength, then we can endure anything. Yes, anything.

O Lord, You see my strength for what it is: puny, unsustainable, ineffective under the present load. As a result, I see my need for two miracles—not just the one that resolves my situation, but a second miracle in my heart so I will allow Your divine power to infuse my life with supernatural endurance. Lord, I must have both miracles. And the miracle of Your enduring strength is one I need now. Thank You, Lord, for Your sufficiency in light of my own insufficiency.

THE 400-YEAR CRY

*The LORD said [to Moses], "I have surely seen the
affliction of my people who are in Egypt and have
heard their cry because of their taskmasters. I
know their sufferings, and I have come down to
deliver them out of the hand of the Egyptians."*

EXODUS 3:7-8

God's people were in bondage. They had been under
the cruel hand of their Egyptian masters for four
centuries. Though they cried out to God, there seemed
to be no answer, no miracle. But God had heard their
cries. God was preparing His Moses for the coming
series of miracles that would bring freedom to His
oppressed people.

If there is to be a Moses to lead you out of your crisis, please know that God will prepare him for the task
ahead. If your miracle doesn't take the form of a Moses,
then you can still know that the God who heard the
centuries-long cries of His people certainly hears your
cries. The miracle is being prepared.

Lord, some days it seems like I've been crying out
to You for centuries. My pleas often seem to fall on
deaf ears. But I know that's only because I'm walking
by sight, not by faith. Faith knows what sight cannot
comprehend—that You are always faithful.

God, You know how this situation is oppressing

me, keeping me from having the joyful life I so desperately want. If You are preparing a Moses who will bring answers to me, send him (or her) soon. If the miracle is not to be found in a Moses, I still trust You to prepare a miracle for me.

In Christ

*Blessed be the God and Father of our Lord Jesus
Christ, who has blessed us in Christ with every
spiritual blessing in the heavenly places.*

EPHESIANS 1:3

Where are our spiritual blessings to be found in good times—and in bad times too? They are *all* to be found in Christ. In Him we have all we need. We have wisdom, discernment, confidence, hope, power to wait out suffering…we have all this and more *in Christ*. Turn to Him for your every need as you pray for your miracle.

Father, thank You for freely giving me all I need in Christ. He is not only my Savior, but through Him I'm supplied with all I need as I wait for the miraculous resolution to my troubles. Lord, use this time to draw me closer to You, to Your Son, and to the Holy Spirit.

As I search Scripture to discover more riches in Christ, may Your Spirit prompt me to recognize when I come upon a fresh supply from Your Word. Thank You most of all that no matter what course my future takes, I'm fully and forever "in Christ."

REIGNING IN LIFE

*If, because of one man's trespass, death reigned through
that one man, much more will those who receive the
abundance of grace and the free gift of righteousness
reign in life through the one man Jesus Christ.*
ROMANS 5:17

We are called to "reign in life." But when trouble
comes, it's hard to see ourselves reigning over
adverse circumstances or the determined will of others
who bring turmoil into our lives. That's when we most
need to reign in life; we need desperately to be overcom-
ers in our prayers, asking *boldly* for our miracle. In short,
we need to get out from under the burdensome pile and
get on top of our circumstances by praying, praying,
praying mightily for the miracle that will bring this era
of life to a close. Reign!

Father, my present circumstances seem to find me
under a pile, far from reigning in life as Your Word
encourages. So, Lord, empower me to get out from
under the load and, through mighty praying and
building faith, rise to the top, where I can once again
reign in life. May my reigning, my prayers, and my
trust in You allow me to soon receive the miracle I
need.

He giveth more grace when the burdens grow greater;
He sendeth more strength when the labors increase.

To added affliction He addeth His mercy;
to multiplied trials, His multiplied peace.

When we have exhausted our store of endurance,
when our strength has failed ere the day is half done,
when we reach the end of our hoarded resources,
our Father's full giving is only begun.

Fear not that thy need shall exceed His provision,
our God ever yearns His resources to share;
lean hard on the arm everlasting, availing;
the Father both thee and thy load will upbear.

His love has no limit; His grace has no measure;
His power no boundary known unto men;
for out of His infinite riches in Jesus,
He giveth, and giveth, and giveth again.
ANNIE JOHNSON FLINT (1866–1932)

GRATITUDE

*Let us be grateful for receiving a kingdom that
cannot be shaken, and thus let us offer to God
acceptable worship, with reverence and awe.*

HEBREWS 12:28

Being grateful to God can be hard when we're surrounded by adversity. Whether our situation is one enormous problem or several small- to medium-sized difficulties, we see little for which we can be thankful. And yet, God calls us to be a grateful people. Even in adversity, we need to remain steadfastly grateful to God for His work in our life. Gratitude is the highway to recognizing more blessings—and receiving our miracle.

Lord, forgive me for my lack of gratefulness. I know I have much for which to be thankful. So I thank You for life itself. I praise You for eternal life to come. I honor You for Your presence in my life now, this very day, in this adverse circumstance. I'm grateful that You have a miracle with my name on it. You will bring to pass Your perfect will and one day deliver me from my present troubles. I wait on You, Father.

REFUSE NEGATIVE THOUGHTS (AND SPEECH)

*It is not what goes into the mouth that defiles a person,
but what comes out of the mouth; this defiles a person.*

MATTHEW 15:11

Faith must be fed daily. It must be nourished by prayer, the Word, and confidence in God. Faith cannot survive long when fed noxious thoughts that lead to counterproductive speech. Negativity feeds doubt. When tempted to think or speak negatively about your trial, force yourself to focus instead on God's faithfulness. Feed faith. Starve doubt.

Lord, doubts come to me too easily, and often I speak those doubts to others. Sometimes I worry about my situation and even envision it becoming worse, not better. Then I give voice to my negative thoughts. If not through my literal voice, then through my inner voice that whispers doubt into my mind.

Father, help me as I search the Word for faith-building promises to feed my thought life. Lead me in prayer as I continually commit my life's issues to You. May the words coming out of my mouth reflect a positive faith in Your power to change my circumstances.

IF YOU HAVE GOD,
YOU HAVE ALL YOU NEED

*My God will supply every need of yours according
to his riches in glory in Christ Jesus.*

PHILIPPIANS 4:19

If you belong to God, you have a provider who gives you all you need. You must, however, "walk by faith, not by sight" (2 Corinthians 5:7). Trust Him to supply your every need—even the very thing that worries you most right now. *He has this.*

Lord, regardless of what I *don't* have, I *do* have You. And you, Father, are enough. Thank You for the ways You provide for me. Thank You that You have this present issue under Your watchful eye. Your provision is enough. Give me eyes to see Your abundance. Allow me to watch as You bring resolution to my present trouble. Lord, I bask in Your riches—all of which are mine to partake. Praise Your name, Father!

God's Good Work in You

I am sure of this, that he who began a good work in you
will bring it to completion at the day of Jesus Christ.

Philippians 1:6

When God's at work, the only possible result is completion. God never starts something He doesn't finish. Right now, you may look at your situation and wonder how God can bring it to a satisfactory end. But you must trust God and wait on Him. He has begun a good work in you, and that work will continue, even as you go through your trial. In fact, your trial will become part of your history with God.

Lord, I know by faith that the work You began in me will continue until "the day of Jesus Christ." You care about me that much. So now, as I wait for a divine resolution to my hard situation, I trust that even this is part of the work that must be done. I pray that good fruit will come from this situation, even though I can't see it now. Father, I pray for the day I can look back and see that You were good to me in my hardest trials.

ABANDONMENT TO GOD

Submit yourselves therefore to God. Resist
the devil, and he will flee from you.
JAMES 4:7

One of the few good things about our trials is the way they force us to let go of our own limited resources and throw ourselves with abandon on God. More trials mean more dependence on God. The more severe the trial, the more our faith is exercised and strengthened. For that we can be thankful.

Father, every trial I go through simply reminds me of my own limitations. I cannot change my present circumstances. It's not within my power to bring about the necessary miracle that will resolve this mess. But in coming to the end of my powers, I find myself joyfully abandoning myself to Your rich resources. Pour out Your answer in great power, Lord. Show Your might on my behalf. Hear my prayer today of utter abandonment to You. You are my hope.

WALK ON WATER

Peter answered him, "Lord, if it is you, command me to come to you on the water." He said, "Come." So Peter got out of the boat and walked on the water and came to Jesus.

MATTHEW 14:28-29

Because of your present dilemma, you're called to walk on water like Peter. In this account in Matthew, we're told that at this time the boat "was a long way from the land, beaten by the waves, for the wind was against them" (verse 24). That's much like us during our hard times. And it was then, not when the waters were calm, that Jesus called Peter to walk on water. Peter obeyed the Lord, stepped out of the boat, and took a few steps toward the Master. But then he looked away from Christ and saw the waters, felt the wind, and began to sink. So, too, we begin to sink as we look at troubles, instead of keeping our eyes fixed on Jesus, who still says, "Come to Me."

Father, staying in the boat during this storm seems so much safer than venturing out on uncertain waters. But due to my present situation, I hear You beckon me to come to You, urging me to believe in the miracle of walking on the raging, stormy waters.

I come, Lord—yes, with some trepidation, but with my eyes fixed on You. Hold out Your hand, Jesus. Steady me. Catch me when I slip toward doubt. Keep me above the roiling waves with Your firm grasp.

Trial is the fruitful soil of trust. Difficulties are the divine incentives which demand and develop our confidence in the divine faithfulness and love... It is so easy for us to lean upon the things that we can see and feel that it is an entirely new experience for us to stand alone and walk with the unseen God as Peter walked upon the sea. But it is a lesson we must learn if we are ever to dwell in the eternal realm, where faith shall be our only sense and God shall be our All in all. Very gently does He suit the test to our feeble strength, and lead us on as we are able from more to more.

A.B. Simpson (1843–1919)

Walking by Faith, Not by Sight

Jesus spoke to them, saying, "I am the light of the world. Whoever follows me will not walk in darkness, but will have the light of life."

JOHN 8:12

When you're in utter darkness, it's hard to find your way along the path. You stumble over rocks. You miss the slight curve to the left the path takes. You bump into the unseen tree. That's the way it is in the spiritual life too. We walk in darkness, but then the light of faith comes into our life, illuminating the path with all its bumps, curves, and obstacles. Today, if you find yourself walking in darkness—seeing no way out of your situation—then turn on the light of faith and walk the path with ease.

Dear Lord, sometimes the path seems so dark. I bump into unseen obstacles. Worse, in the darkness, I can't see the road ahead. I can't see where I'm going or the goal at the end of the path. Please, Father, help me as I learn to walk this journey by faith, not by sight. For faith, when exercised, becomes light on my path.

In the light of faith, I discern the road ahead. I see the goal and continue toward it. Lord, light my way.

In Your Weakness

He said to me, "My grace is sufficient for you, for
my power is made perfect in weakness." Therefore I
will boast all the more gladly of my weaknesses, so
that the power of Christ may rest upon me.

2 Corinthians 12:9

It's one of the upside-down principles of God's kingdom that when we're weak, we're actually strong. When we're poor, we're rich. To those who don't know the Lord, it sounds like foolishness. But we understand that in our weakness, we are empowered by His strength.

Let weakness become your ally as it forces you to be filled with the divine strength God gives. With Paul, boast gladly about your weakness, so that the power of Christ may rest upon you.

O Lord, my God, I am so weak! In many ways, I'm also poor. I'm thankful that my weakness and poverty are really doorways to enter into Your strength and riches. Lord, I boast of my weakness as I invite You to be my strength. Become my riches. May my life overflow with Your presence and power.

Lord, if I don't have Your strength, I have nothing. Thank You for never failing to freely give Your power to the powerless. For giving your power to me.

The Mighty Hand of God

*Humble yourselves, therefore, under the mighty hand
of God so that at the proper time he may exalt you.*
1 Peter 5:6

God's hands are mighty. He can move mountains, even the one you're facing right now. Trust in the power of God—and nothing less—to get you through this troubling time.

O Lord, sometimes I forget just how mighty You are. Nothing is too difficult for You. Your arms are mighty. Your hand reaches all the way from heaven right into my life with its current discord.

Your hand, moved by Your loving heart, brings peace, restoration, and healing. Father, show forth Your strength on my behalf. Bring about the miracle I so desperately need. I trust in Your mighty hands!

GOD OF THE IMPOSSIBLE

Behold, I am the LORD, the God of all
flesh. Is anything too hard for me?
JEREMIAH 32:27

A miracle is necessary only when we're facing the impossible. If we can fix the situation ourselves, there's no need for a miracle. But when the impossible is called for, God must step in. For with God, nothing, absolutely *nothing*, is impossible.

Father God, I believe that with You, nothing is impossible. The word doesn't exist in Your dictionary. However, in my present dictionary, it's in blazing capital letters.

Yes, Lord, what I'm in the middle of seems impossible to me. There simply is no human way to fix this. But *You*, Lord, can bring about the circumstances, the right people, the perfect timing to remedy my situation. God, let me see with my own eyes as You perform the impossible in my life. I will give You the praise *forever*. I will tell others of Your greatness and Your care for me.

Praying with Authority

Peter said, "I have no silver and gold, but what I do have
I give to you. In the name of Jesus Christ of Nazareth,
rise up and walk!"...And leaping up, [the lame man]
stood and began to walk, and entered the temple
with them, walking and leaping and praising God.
ACTS 3:6-8

Just as there are short prayers, such as we find in this book, and longer prayers when we're having an extended time before the Lord, so, too, there are prayers that come from our weakness and also prayers that come from our strength in Christ. The former are often as simple as "Help, Lord!" The latter are usually birthed out of an understanding of our authority in Christ. We can and often *must* pray with authority.

Peter and John met a lame beggar outside the temple. His condition was impossible with man. But they knew their authority in Christ and prayed boldly for a miracle. And God came through.

Ask God to build up within you the capability to pray with great authority. He will use you mightily as one of His prayer warriors.

Lord, You have given me a measure of authority as a believer in Christ. Teach me to wield this authority in prayer so that I can see victory in my own circumstances and help others find freedom too. Father,

71

open my eyes to the scriptures that affirm my authority. Bring about life-changing results as I practice praying this way. May I understand that authority also comes with holiness of life. Increase, then, Lord, my hunger for true personal holiness.

Obey What You Know to Do

Whoever knows the right thing to do and
fails to do it, for him it is sin.
JAMES 4:17

We often find ourselves in trouble because we did something we shouldn't have done, or we didn't do something we should have. As for your present situation, is there something you need to do that will help bring resolution? Perhaps it's something you dread doing, but you know you must. If so, then do it and hasten the ending of your trial.

Lord, is there anything I need to do to help bring about the miracle of restoration in my life? Is there anyone to whom I must make amends? Is there an unresolved financial matter I need to clear up? Is there a habit I must end that will bring relief to my situation? Lord, I want to obey You in all things. If there is any disobedience in my life, please show me, and I will attend to it at once.

Be assured, if you walk with Him and look to Him,
and expect help from Him, He will never fail you.
GEORGE MUELLER (1805–1898)

You Cannot Be Shaken

He only is my rock and my salvation,
my fortress; I shall not be shaken.

Psalm 62:6

The longer our situation goes on, the more likely we're going to feel shaken in our faith. *Will God come through? Am I wasting my time trusting Him to do something? Shouldn't I just give up?*

When going through a severe trial requiring a miracle, we must be resilient. We must become strong and remain strong. Nothing must be allowed to shake our faith.

Do not be shaken by your adversity. Persevere!

Lord, this is taking so long. I feel like I'm being shaken to my very core. Help me, Father, become unshakable, no matter how long it takes for this circumstance to be resolved. Use this time to help me put down firm roots that anchor me to the ground of faith. May I become the person who can withstand any storm, no matter how intense or how long it endures. Yes, Lord, make me unshakable.

GIVE THANKS IN ALL CIRCUMSTANCES

*Give thanks in all circumstances; for this is
the will of God in Christ Jesus for you.*
1 THESSALONIANS 5:18

Is it possible to give thanks "in all circumstances"? Even in *this*?

Yes, even in this. You'll find that thankfulness itself is its own reward. Don't accept bitterness, anger, or discouragement as your attitude. Become thankful and remain thankful—in *all* things.

Father, You know how hard it can be to give thanks in all things. Especially in *this*. But I remain confident that You will bring relief to me. I repent of my lack of thankfulness, and I resolve to thank You now, ahead of time, for the miracle that's coming my way.

Whenever I lapse into self-pity or some other negative mood, turn my thoughts toward thankfulness as a more productive mind-set. Right now, Lord, I take a moment to explicitly thank You for loving me and for providing the coming resolution to my trial.

DELIGHT YOURSELF IN THE LORD

Delight yourself in the LORD,
and he will give you the desires of your heart.

PSALM 37:4

We should, at all times, delight ourselves in God. Not only for the joy of doing so, but because of the promise that comes with it: "He will give you the desires of your heart." What incentive! But please, don't rejoice in God just for what it will bring you. Delight yourself in Him because of who He is. The resulting joy is like having dessert after a satisfying meal.

O God, how easy it is to delight myself in You. You are a true bringer of joy to my heart. Hear my praises as I come to You with sheer delight and awesome wonder at Your character, Your power, and Your unending love for me.

May delighting in You become my daily habit, starting each morning and remaining my attitude until I go to bed at night. Lord, You are delightful! Even in the middle of my situation, I *still* will delight in You—now and always.

Natural or Supernatural?

*No longer drink only water, but use a little wine for
the sake of your stomach and your frequent ailments.*
1 Timothy 5:23

We often think of a miracle as God's supernatural move in an impossible situation. And that's true. But it's also true that God often moves in our lives through natural means. For example, if we're seriously ill, God may heal us supernaturally…or He may lead us to the right doctor who can help us by prescribing a natural cure for our sickness.

In the New Testament case of Timothy, Paul recommended a little wine for Timothy's "frequent ailments." That was a natural remedy. So don't limit how God will work in your situation. Allow Him to move supernaturally or naturally. Either one can be a miracle.

Dear Lord, I'm so in need of a miracle, and I don't care if You move supernaturally or if You bring a miraculous remedy through natural means. I don't care if the remedy is fast or slow. I don't care if it's through a person, a dream, or some unlikely agency. I will keep an open mind, Lord, and watch You work however You choose…and I will praise You for it, in any case.

*Four things let us ever keep in mind: God
hears prayer, God heeds prayer, God answers
prayer, and God delivers by prayer.*
E.M. Bounds (1835–1913)

NOT BY MIGHT, NOR BY POWER

[The angel] said to me, "This is the word of the
LORD to Zerubbabel: Not by might, nor by power,
but by my Spirit, says the LORD of hosts."
ZECHARIAH 4:6

God moves by His Spirit—not by might, nor by power. Relinquish any hopes for *your* might to bring resolution. Surrender your puny power to alter the situation. Trust in His Spirit to accomplish what you cannot.

Father God, Your Spirit can do the impossible. I cannot. I have no might nor power to fix my present circumstance. Lord, come through for me as only You can do. Bring forth *Your* might, release *Your* power. Move by Your Spirit to accomplish a great thing here. Remove every obstacle. Turn away every attempt by the enemy or a third person to only make the situation worse. Move by Your Spirit, Lord!

RESIST EVIL IN EVERY FORM

The fear of the LORD is hatred of evil.

PROVERBS 8:13

If there's an element of evil in our trial, it must be resisted. There is great power in resistance. Too often, we become passive or are simply ignorant regarding evil and how to deal with it. Evil is never to be tolerated, and removing or resisting any evil influence in our present crisis might hasten the miracle of restoration.

Lord, make me aware of any evil element in my present crisis. Help me stand strong as I firmly resist it. Strengthen me as I turn away the corrupt influences—whether they be spiritual powers or actual evil persons wreaking havoc in my life. Empower me with truths from Your Word that will help me in my resistance. Bring to mind the verses that speak of my spiritual armor and the weapons of my warfare.

In Christ's name, I do resist and renounce every evil influence in my life.

Treasure God's Answer

I will give you the treasures of darkness
and the hoards in secret places,
that you may know that it is I, the Lord,
the God of Israel, who call you by your name.

Isaiah 45:3

God doesn't do miracles just for show. Every miracle has a purpose, just as every trial has a desired end from God's point of view. When the answer arrives, God means for us to remember in the future how He moved on our behalf. He wants us to treasure the miracle that comes. It is, after all, a gift from God.

Just as the Old Testament Jews set up physical memorials to God's faithfulness along the way through the desert, so should we treasure the miracles of God that happen in our life. During future trials, it will bring confidence for us to recall God's faithfulness in our past trials.

God, You know I'm so in need of a miracle that when it comes, I will give You praise and honor. I will be thankful forever. And I will treasure Your answer, no matter what it is, for it will bring Your desired resolution to my trial.

In my heart, I will build a memorial to remind me that at this place and at this time, my Lord came through for me and brought the miracle I needed.

Changing Your Mind

Set your minds on things that are above,
not on things that are on earth.

COLOSSIANS 3:2

One of the first steps in experiencing a miracle is to change our mind about our situation and also our perception of God and what He can do for us. We must believe that God is moving in our life *all the time*. God is never *not* at work. Every circumstance has a desired outcome from God's point of view. He uses everything and wastes nothing.

Lord, my situation causes me to worry about the outcome of my trial. I seem to focus only on the trouble and not on Your solution. Help me change my mind and realize that even during this hard time, You're working on my behalf. You have a planned outcome for me, and I must focus on that instead of my present crisis.

Father, You use everything and waste nothing. I pray, then, for You to use this hard trial for my eventual good.

GOD ISN'T WORRIED

Which of you by being anxious can add
a single hour to his span of life?
MATTHEW 6:27

Know that God is not worried about your situation. He is not surprised at the way things have fallen out so far, and He sees what's ahead for you. What He asks of you now is to trust—*utterly trust*—in Him. Place yourself and your situation in God's care, and then leave it there.

Father, I'm comforted by the realization that You know the future. You're already there, at the very day my situation is resolved. You see the perfect outcome according to Your plan.

Lord, though You're not worried about what's ahead, I still have days when I feel anxious and uncertain. Help me, Lord, to cast my worries aside...to cast my anxieties on You, knowing You can handle them all. Praise Your name!

The "Why Me?" Question

Though he slay me, I will hope in him.
Job 13:15

During our darkest days, we may wonder, *Why is this happening to me? Is it something I've done…or not done?* We may even point to our past obedience to God and declare, "I don't deserve this trial!" We know Job felt that way, and yet, in the end, he could hope in God, even should He slay him.

It's puzzling when God doesn't answer the "Why me?" question. He leaves it for us to approach our circumstances by faith, not by sight.

Leave the "Why me?" question behind. You won't find out the answer this side of heaven—and when you get right down to it, if you're willing to live by faith, the *why* doesn't really matter, does it?

Father, it has crossed my mind to ask, "Why me?" If I had been allowed to map out my life's path, I would have spared myself this agony. But You have chosen instead to let me walk this dark path. Lord, give me strength for each step. Help me get past the questioning phase of my trial. Strengthen me so I no longer ask when or how the miracle will come. Allow me to fully rest in the knowledge of Your goodness—from which shall come my miracle in due time.

BUT IF NOT...

If this be so, our God whom we serve is able to deliver us from the burning fiery furnace, and he will deliver us out of your hand, O king. But if not, be it known to you, O king, that we will not serve your gods or worship the golden image that you have set up.

DANIEL 3:17-18

In the book of Daniel, we read of Shadrach, Meshach, and Abednego, who, when ordered to worship the golden image set up by Nebuchadnezzar under threat of being cast into the fiery furnace, gave the answer in today's passage.

The three men were then cast into the furnace. They did not escape the fire. But, praise God, they did not go through the fire alone. After heating up the furnace seven times hotter than usual, Nebuchadnezzar exclaimed, "I see four men unbound, walking in the midst of the fire, and they are not hurt; and the appearance of the fourth is like a son of the gods" (verse 25). Ah yes. *The* Son of God was in the furnace with them. They came out so unscathed that not even the odor of smoke was upon them.

You, too, have another person in the furnace with you. You, too, might come out unscathed, protected by God. *But if not,* you, like the three men of God, will not desert your heavenly Father. Stay the course. Endure the furnace with the Son of God beside you.

Father, this trial is surely a fiery furnace. I fear coming out burned to a crisp. Yet I look at how You sent Your Son into the furnace with Shadrach, Meshach, and Abednego and kept them alive through the heat of the furnace. O Lord, I feel the furnace heating up. I see the flames licking at my heels. I must have Jesus with me until I'm removed from the fire. Until then, thank You for the presence of Jesus in the fire with me.

Prayer and the Promises of God

*Fully convinced that God was able
to do what he had promised.*

Romans 4:21

The way we learn to have faith in God for our difficult situation is to consider the Bible as a container of God's promises to His people. It's by faith in His promises that we advance in the Christian life. It's through faith in God and His promises that we will receive our miracle. What promise from God's Word is your anchor today? Are you "fully convinced" He can fulfill it?

Wow, God, Your promises are the bedrock of my life. Daily I live by Your promises—and when I leave Earth, I have the promise of eternity with You. Awesome!

Lord, You know full well when I need to find a fresh promise to lean on. Continue to open Your Word to me and fill my mind with the amazing promises found there. Renew my mind—my way of thinking—with Your infallible Word.

Stay my mind on each relevant promise You guide me to in the Bible.

I will hold each one close to my heart.

Affliction is often that thing which prepares an ordinary person for some sort of an extraordinary destiny.
C.S. Lewis (1898–1963)

GOD *ALWAYS* COMES THROUGH

*Know therefore that the LORD your God is
God, the faithful God who keeps covenant and
steadfast love with those who love him and keep
his commandments, to a thousand generations.*

DEUTERONOMY 7:9

Of course, God always comes through. And if for the first time in history God doesn't come through, then it's on Him. Faith is our guarantee that God will come through. Faith in His promises always delivers... in God's way and in God's time.

Dear Lord, You are never-failing. You always come through for Your people. There isn't a need we have that You can't fill. Even our wants are often Your delight to deliver.

Father, I know You're going to come through in my present situation. I know, by faith, You will send Your miracle in Your time. Until then, I pray this will continue to be a faith-building time for me. Let not one day go to waste through needless worry. Lord, You are faithful!

FOLLOW PRAYER WITH PRAISE

I will sing to the LORD as long as I live;
I will sing praise to my God while I have being.
PSALM 104:33

The challenge for many people is that they feel they *can't* praise God in their current circumstance. Sure, when God "comes through" the way they expect, and their problem is in the past, they'll rejoice and praise God till they have no more breath. Until then, praise seems hard, often hollow. But *now*, in the midst of your trial, is the time to praise Him.

Let today be a "praise day" while you consider God's intervention in your problem.

Lord, first I pray again for the solution to my situation. I thank You for the soon-coming miracle. But now I choose to follow up my prayer with a time of praise. Not because You will send a miracle, but simply because I love You, no matter how this all falls out.

Yes, Lord, I praise You now with a full heart and a ready tongue. I worship You, Father. I extol You and lift up Your name. You, Lord, are worthy to be praised!

Empowerment from on High

Summon your power, O God,
the power, O God, by which you have worked for us.
PSALM 68:28

What if God's miraculous resolution to your situation is not a removal of the trial, but an empowerment from on high that allows you to overcome the obstacles in your way? Can you handle that? We know God does give us strength for every battle, and we should also know that His strength always outlasts the battle.

Draw power from God today. Be empowered.

Lord, summon Your power by which You work for us! Endue me with a strength beyond my natural strength. Allow me to stand strong in Your might as I face the giants in my life. May Your supernatural power outlast this and every trial that comes my way. Holy Spirit, strengthen me. Abide in me. Guide me. Empower me.

Your Words Count

*The good person out of the good treasure of his
heart produces good, and the evil person out
of his evil treasure produces evil, for out of the
abundance of the heart his mouth speaks.*

LUKE 6:45

Jesus often spoke about the importance of the words coming out of our mouth. So did Paul. So did David and Solomon in both Psalms and Proverbs. When we're in a rough patch, waiting for a miracle, we must not let our mouth defy us by speaking doubt and negativity into an already bad situation. Speak faith and positivity, not based on anything reasonable, but on your faith in God.

Speak it!

O God, I do need to guard my mouth at all times. I must not speak doubt and negativity into my life. Help me recall promises from Your Word to speak into my troubling situations. Make my mouth a fountain of good, not of evil or doubting. Allow my words to come into alignment with Your perfect will.

Mouth: speak truth, not doubt!

Welcome Trials

Count it all joy, my brothers, when you meet
trials of various kinds, for you know that the
testing of your faith produces steadfastness. And
let steadfastness have its full effect, that you may
be perfect and complete, lacking in nothing.

James 1:2-4

When we're at our lowest, it's hard to think of a severe trial as something to welcome, yet that's what the apostle James tells us to do. The goal, of course, is that as we endure our trials, we learn to persevere. Our faith is enabled to grow. Welcome this present chance to trust God and see His hand move in your circumstance.

Father, to welcome this trial, I must do so through gritted teeth. It's hard for me to imagine how this situation can be of any benefit. Even so, Lord, to the best of my ability, I welcome this opportunity to see Your hand at work. I pray that I will learn more about endurance as this present trouble continues to unfold and move toward Your designed resolution.

Lord, I look for the good fruit in my life to come out of this ordeal.

When You Must Wait

I believe that I shall look upon the goodness of the LORD
in the land of the living!
Wait for the LORD;
be strong, and let your heart take courage;
wait for the LORD!
PSALM 27:13-14

Miracles can be fast or slow. Jesus performed many "fast" miracles when He walked among us. But God also does slower miracles. He ordains circumstances to change over time. Slowly. That means waiting. You may say, "But I don't have time for a slow miracle. My situation demands an immediate solution." God knows this. But He works on His timetable, not ours.

Father, waiting is hard. My timetable calls for a quick miracle, a rapid resolution. Your timetable is slower than mine. Help me accept with patience the slow revealing of Your will, Lord. Still my mind when it rushes ahead to propose all sorts of ways for my miracle to come. Help me accept not only Your timetable, but Your miracle, not mine.

ACCEPTING GOD'S MIRACLE

Your kingdom come,
your will be done,
on earth as it is in heaven.
MATTHEW 6:10

Will we recognize God's miracle when it comes? We have our own idea of the miracle, but we must be looking for God's creative ways of bringing it about—and be thankful when it comes. We must want, above all, for His will to be done on earth. *His* will, not ours.

Rest assured, your miracle is on its way…but it may not look like the miracle you anticipated. Instead, it is one that reflects God's will being done on earth as it is in heaven.

Give me eyes to see, O Lord, when my miracle comes. Allow me to lay down my expectations of the miracle You'll send. Help me understand how Your answer is the perfect answer. Give me peace that passes understanding as I receive Your miracle. May great blessing come from this present desperate situation. Most of all, may Your will be done on earth as it is in heaven.

KNOCKING

Ask, and it will be given to you; seek, and you will find; knock, and it will be opened to you. For everyone who asks receives, and the one who seeks finds, and to the one who knocks it will be opened.

MATTHEW 7:7-8

In the verse above, Jesus talked about the importance of "knocking." To have God answer our prayers, we must knock…and knock…and knock some more. The casual light tap on the door doesn't get the miracle. It's the persistent knocking that brings the sleeping man down to give bread to his neighbor (see Luke 11:5-10). The miracle comes to those who knock, seek, and *find*.

Lord, do You hear me knocking? I have come to You in urgency and seek Your attention in my desperate matter. Father, I know You will hear the persistent knocking of Your child. I know You will open the door and give me bread. You will hear and come to me and be with me in my dilemma.

Father, I will not stop knocking until I have Your answer.

GOD'S CLOCK

I trust in you, O LORD;
I say, "You are my God."
My times are in your hand;
rescue me from the hand of my enemies
and from my persecutors!

PSALM 31:14-15

Do you sometimes wonder if God's clock is broken? Or at least running slow? But no, God's clock is always on time…always right. Turn away from glancing at your own clock and look instead to God's timepiece. Trust His timing.

Father, sometimes I think Your clock is running slow. My watch says it's time for the immediate resolution of my situation. But then, my watch always runs fast. Help me, Lord, to wait on You. Help me keep my eyes on Your clock.

May the minutes and hours tick by at Your speed. Give me understanding of Your timing.

PRAYING FOR OTHERS

*Praying at all times in the Spirit, with all prayer
and supplication. To that end, keep alert with all
perseverance, making supplication for all the saints.*

EPHESIANS 6:18

Many other people have this same book in their possession. Each one has a problem that's as serious to them as yours is to you. Can I suggest that you take a break from praying for your own miracle today and, instead, pray for other readers of this book, wherever they are? You can know that as others read this page, they're praying for you.

Father, it's human nature that our own problems always seem to loom larger in our life than the crises others are facing. Today, I want to lift up other readers of this book, wherever they are. I don't know their situation, but You do. Please, God, bring them the miracle they need speedily. Comfort them as they wait. Bless their very hard situation and turn it to good. Thank You, Lord, that You hear my prayer for them and their prayers for me.

STOP TRYING TO
FIGURE IT OUT

The LORD will fight for you, and you have only to be silent.
EXODUS 14:14

When confronted with an impossible situation, most of us try to figure out a natural solution. Then, when the circumstances don't comport with our plan, we come up with another way it could possibly work out. All the while, we could save all that angst and mental gymnastics by ceasing our own efforts to bring about a solution and simply waiting on God for His answer…His miracle.

Father, my mind comes up with so many plans and solutions to my problem. They seldom work out, though. So instead, Lord, I'm going to be silent, stop all this mental maneuvering, and wait on You for an answer. Your power to design answers to impossible situations trumps my puny abilities. Your promise to fight for me assures me of victory.

Lord, I present my problem to You…again. Come up with Your answer, please.

*I know not what He is about to do with me, but
I have given myself entirely into His hands.*
CATHERINE BOOTH (1829–1890)

What Can You Learn?

Let the wise hear and increase in learning,
and the one who understands obtain guidance.

Proverbs 1:5

Within each trial—no matter how severe—there's something for us to discover, perhaps a lesson to be learned. Sometimes we must wait for a hidden blessing that will appear at the right time.

While we pray for our miracle, let's also keep our eyes open for something good that will come from our trial, even it's simply that we're learning how fully we must trust God in all things. Even in this.

God, it's hard to think about any good coming from my situation. There can be no blessing in this trial...or can there? If so, Lord, help me find it. Open my eyes to see the lesson, to discern the hidden blessing, to perceive how dependent on You I must be. Father, reveal Your intent for me during this rough season.

His Active Love

Give thanks to the God of heaven,
for his steadfast love endures forever.
Psalm 136:26

One of the greatest miracles to ponder is God's amazing and steadfast love for us. When we're in the deep woods of affliction, we may temporarily doubt God's love, or perhaps we just see it a bit more dimly than when things are going well. But we each must know that today, in this very hour of affliction, God's love for us is profound, unchanging, and *active*.

God, Your love for me is a perfect and eternal love. It's active and unstoppable.

Lord, I take a moment now to consider the depth of Your love for me. During this current affliction, though I have not doubted Your love, I've let it become merely knowledge instead of experience in my life.

Father, may Your love envelop me today, and may it hasten the miracle I so desperately need.

In times of affliction we commonly meet with
the sweetest experiences of the love of God.
John Bunyan (1628–1688)

God, the Great Giver

Every good gift and every perfect gift is from above,
coming down from the Father of lights, with whom
there is no variation or shadow due to change.

JAMES 1:17

God is first, last, and always a giver. He gave His Son for us. Daily He gives us life. In eternity, He gives us heaven. Now, in our current predicament, we have to believe He gives us miracles as we need them. Trust God's giving nature with which there is no variation or shadow of change.

Father, thank You for all You give me: life, family, daily bread, Your Son, and eventually, heaven. Lord, I also thank You in advance for the miracle that is now on its way to remedy my situation. It is Your gift to me.

God, You love to give. I thank You for this present opportunity to receive a miracle from You. I praise You, Lord, for Your love and Your giving nature.

THE BLESSING OF GIVING

It is more blessed to give than to receive.
ACTS 20:35

Just as God is a giver, we must also be generous. One of the basics of the Christian message is that it's "more blessed to give than to receive." Even though we want to receive as we offer these prayers, we must also be mindful of being generous givers. We may give our time to the lonely, financial aid to the needy, a warm meal to a sick friend. Whatever we have to give to someone undergoing difficulty results in a blessing for us—a larger blessing than receiving. It's also a demonstration of Jesus's words in Matthew 7:12, "Whatever you wish that others would do to you, do also to them."

Father, as I watch for my miracle, I realize that giving is more important than receiving. Help me learn to emulate You in giving. May I open my eyes to the needs around me. If remotely possible, help me be the miracle someone else needs. Make me aware of those to whom I can give in order to bring blessing into their lives.

Lord, as I give, may my own dire circumstances become dimmer in light of the ways I can bless others. Because of Your generosity to me, I can be generous to others.

CALL FOR THE ELDERS

*Is anyone among you sick? Let him call for the
elders of the church, and let them pray over him,
anointing him with oil in the name of the Lord.*

JAMES 5:14

Do you have a good church family? Are there elders
in your church whom you can trust with your present need, even if your trial doesn't involve sickness? God
has established elders in the church to guide us, advise
us, comfort us, and pray for us. Don't neglect this vital
element in every believer's life. Your miracle may come
from God through a trusted church leader.

Father, You know my church situation. Right now, I
pray for those in leadership in my church. Give me
the courage to include them in my quest for a miracle.
Then give them the compassion required of an elder
to shepherd me during this hard time.

If they offer advice, Lord, I pray that it will be
prompted by Your Spirit. Give me the wisdom to discern their words and the courage to act on what they
say if it's a word from You. If the elders are not able
to help me, Father, lead me to other wise men and
women who can shepherd me during these hard
days. Lord, this sheep needs help.

WHERE TWO OR THREE ARE GATHERED

If two of you agree on earth about anything they ask, it will be done for them by my Father in heaven. For where two or three are gathered in my name, there am I among them.

MATTHEW 18:19-20

No one should carry a heavy burden alone. Do you have others joining you in prayer? Are you keeping them informed about changes in your situation? God will send warriors to stand with you, if you will ask.

Father God, though there is power in one person praying, You encourage us to pray in twos and threes—that is, You want us to seek You together as well as individually. Lord, I know I can't bear this burden alone, so I pray now for at least two or three others whom I can trust to keep a confidence. I pray You'll put on my heart just the right people to ask. Then, as I share with them, I pray they'll fully see my burden and take it as their own. Father, use my prayers and those of my prayer team to bring about the deep change—the miracle—that will end my situation.

In Light of Eternity

Blessed be the LORD, the God of Israel,
from everlasting to everlasting!
PSALM 41:13

No question about it: Our problems are significant. Even life-changing. But no matter how earth-moving our predicament, it will eventually pale in light of eternity. Sometimes it helps to remember this. It's likely that in only a few years, what we're going through will be a memory—a memory of when God came through for us. So, yes, our problem is huge. It's significant. It's earthshaking. But it's also temporary. God will move on your behalf, and this pain will fade into the past. See your situation today in light of eternity.

O Lord, this present problem seems like a huge boulder in the path that is my life's journey. But even so, I realize it will one day no longer exist. You will supply the perfect ending to my situation.

Help me keep my eyes not on the problems of the present, but on the unchangeable and eternal aspects of Your kingdom. In so focusing, may the weight of the burden be shifted away from me.

THE PRESENCE OF THE LORD

The LORD is near to all who call on him,
to all who call on him in truth.

PSALM 145:18

Sometimes, in the midst of our pain, we don't discern the presence of the Lord. We ask, "Where are you, God?" And yet, His presence is always with us, even on our darkest days. He is with you today—now, right where you are. Take comfort.

Dear Father, thank You for being *here*. Thank You that You have vowed never to leave me alone. I take refuge in Your presence. I hide under Your wings. God, I lean hard on You. Bring me fresh awareness of Your ever-present nearness. May Your presence bring me not just comfort, but courage for the days ahead and strength to endure until the miracle has come.

LOOKING BACK

You shall remember that you were a slave in the land of Egypt, and the LORD your God brought you out from there with a mighty hand and an outstretched arm.

DEUTERONOMY 5:15

During our roughest days, it may help to look back and consider our past trials. Were they not resolved? Did God not bring an end to them? Perhaps at the time, we saw no way out…yet with God there was a way, and we eventually came out of the tunnel. Why, then, would God not come through for us again?

He will, of course. Just as He came through for the Hebrew slaves desperate for freedom from the oppressive Egyptians. They, too, needed to be reminded of God's great deliverance with "a mighty hand and an outstretched arm."

Today, recount in your mind a past situation you thought could not be redeemed. In short, celebrate God's past faithfulness as you watch for Him to come through once again. And remember, He is not just the light at the *end* of the tunnel. He's your light while you're *in* the tunnel.

Lord, I can be so shortsighted. I too easily forget Your past presence in my life and trials. Yet, You have always come through for me. No, not necessarily the way I envisioned, but in the way that pleased You the most. So, Father, as I am once again in a dark tunnel, I celebrate Your past victories and look forward to Your triumph at the end of this present tunnel. Like the Hebrew slaves, bring me out of my present sojourn in Egypt. Meanwhile, Lord, may you be my light *in* the tunnel.

Your Broken Places

*The Lord is near to the brokenhearted
and saves the crushed in spirit.*

Psalm 34:18

You've perhaps heard of the Japanese term *kintsugi*. It refers to the ancient practice of taking a piece of treasured broken pottery and repairing it by using a lacquer mixed with a precious medal such as gold to fuse the broken shards together. The result is a more beautiful and stronger vessel.

In our present situation, let's see ourselves as broken vessels in need of the miracle of repair and turn to the master *kintsugi* artist, God. He turns what has been broken into something even more beautiful than the original creation.

Lord, this present crisis has broken me in so many ways. Can You—*will* You—take the broken shards of my life and work the miracle of restoration? Will You bind my pieces back together with precious gold from Your forge? O God, to be fashioned anew by You is my one desire as I face the uncertain future. Lord, make me Your vessel, refashioned by pure gold.

GOD, WHY DID YOU LET THIS HAPPEN?

The LORD blessed the latter days of Job more than his beginning.

JOB 42:12

Who among us during our darkest days has not asked, "God, *why?*" We wonder why this present crisis is upon us. How could a loving Father let this happen? And how can it possibly be resolved? These questions are natural—just ask Job. But when you ask him, remember the end of his story: "The LORD blessed the latter days of Job more than his beginning."

May that be your testimony too.

O Lord, I don't know why this has happened or what You mean to accomplish in my life by it. Right now, it just seems like an awful mess. But then I realize Job had no idea what was going on behind the scenes as his series of tragedies unfolded. If someone could have come to Job and said, "Just wait, everything is going to be okay. In fact, your latter days are bright! You will have more after your tragedies than before," I wonder if he would have believed them.

God, help *me* believe. Help me know by faith that there are things about this situation going on that I really know nothing about. Only You know those details, Lord. I trust You...the God who restores. The God of Job.

IF ONLY

One thing I do: forgetting what lies behind and straining
forward to what lies ahead, I press on toward the goal
for the prize of the upward call of God in Christ Jesus.

PHILIPPIANS 3:13-14

There's one phrase arising from our situation that, when whispered in our ear, is almost always from the enemy of our soul. The phrase begins with, "If only…" As in, *If only I hadn't* _____.
You fill in the blank.

The problem with that phrase is that it's backward looking. "If only" no longer matters. What matters now is that you need God's intervention. That's your new focus. Forget what lies behind. Strain forward to what lies ahead. Press toward the goal.

God, sometimes I'm haunted with if-onlys. I think, *If only I hadn't done such and such.* Or, *If only so-and-so would do what they're supposed to.* Or, *If only this event had taken a different turn.*

Lord, help me get past the if-only syndrome. Help me realize that's a maze without an exit. Instead, Lord, help me focus on the future, not on the past. Bring about the solution, the miracle that will forever silence the if-onlys in my life. Hear me as I press on toward the prize of Your upward call.

Faith-Building Books

When you come, bring the cloak that I left with Carpus
at Troas, also the books, and above all the parchments.
2 Timothy 4:13

The apostle Paul must have loved his books. So much so, he instructed Timothy to bring the ones he had left at Troas.

Many fine Christian authors have written books that can help build your faith in miracles. One of the most amazing is *The Hiding Place* by Corrie ten Boom. Imagine being held in a Nazi prison camp with fleas everywhere. Imagine her praying for the miracle that would eventually set her free to travel the world with the gospel—along with the story of the miracle God provided her. And remember, Corrie's God is your God too.

God, I think of how Corrie ten Boom was at the lowest ebb of her life, and yet, You had an end plan she couldn't see that can only be termed a *miracle*. Lord, You were a father to Corrie and so many others who experienced dramatic turns in life that were surely miracles sent by You.

Today, I pray to You, *my* Father, to bring about the miracle I need in my life. Father, I believe there's no miracle any author has ever written about that couldn't also be my miracle. Bring it on, Lord!

How Trouble Changes You

Before I was afflicted I went astray,
but now I keep your word.

PSALM 119:67

Notice how the psalmist contrasts who he was before he was afflicted versus after his affliction. Your present need will change you, no doubt about it. Let the change be for your good, as that's God's goal with this trial. Let the full work of God be done in your life, even as you endure the pain of waiting. Your day will come.

God, I know You use trials and afflictions to change us. Lord, I see how the change in me could be good or bad, depending on how I handle it. I might become sullen, bitter, and discouraged as I keep waiting for Your resolution. I pray that won't happen. Please keep Your hand on me. Keep me delighting in You, even on the hard days. Bring about the change in me You desire...for if You desire it, then so do I.

The Hem of His Garment

As Jesus went, the people pressed around him. And there was a woman who had had a discharge of blood for twelve years, and though she had spent all her living on physicians, she could not be healed by anyone. She came up behind him and touched the fringe of his garment, and immediately her discharge of blood ceased.

Luke 8:42-44

How much of Jesus did this poor woman need to touch for her miracle? Not much at all. Just the hem of His garment. But the secret to her healing is that she did so with faith.

Will you simply touch the hem of His garment today, spiritually speaking? In other words, will you reach out in prayer, knowing He hears every word? He doesn't strain to hear you, so you need not strain in praying to Him.

Simply pray and believe.

O Lord, You see my amount of faith today. Sometimes it seems high; other days, not so much. But as You are passing by this way today, Lord, I reach out in prayer and simply touch the hem of Your garment. Though You might barely feel the lightness of my touch, You will surely hear the plea of my heart. And just as the woman was healed, so, too, will You bring healing to my situation.

Just to reach out to You, Lord, will accomplish much.

WHEN GOD SAYS NO

*The heart of man plans his way,
but the Lord establishes his steps.*

PROVERBS 16:9

We all have prayed and received a negative answer. And we often question why God said no. A yes would have been much more to our liking. But when God says no to our plea, it's only a no to the resolution *we* want.

God has heard your many prayers regarding your trial and will indeed send a miracle. When God says no to your Plan B, He's really saying yes to His Plan A, which is so much better than our puny plan.

Lord, I hate to receive a no to my specific prayer. But when I do, please help me believe that it's really a yes to something far better. Your zigzags in my life are always aimed at the destination You have chosen for me. My seemingly straight line of yeses would only lead me to a place where You know I'd ultimately be unhappy.

Lord, I'll take every no, as long as I know that it's really Your yes.

Focus on the Future

The Lord will fulfill his purpose for me;
your steadfast love, O Lord, endures forever.
Do not forsake the work of your hands.

Psalm 138:8

No trial lasts forever, though while you're in the midst of it, it may seem that way. You do have a future after this suffering. Even if bad health threatens, you have an eternal destiny in heaven. During the present hard time, it will refresh you to envision the future after this ordeal has come to an end—after God has brought about whatever miracle will resolve the situation. Think about it. Pray about it. Thank God for the very future that He has planned. Allow your mind to skip ahead and, for a time, set aside the present agonies. They *will* pass.

O Lord, thank You for the future You have planned for me. Yes, I know there will be additional trials in my life, but for now, I set aside my worries and look forward to the days when I've finally passed through this valley.

Father, bring about a miracle in Your timing, but I do pray it might be soon. I long to be part of a future with all this present hardship behind me.

God, You are so good to me—all the time.

WISDOM

Get wisdom,
and whatever you get,
get insight.
PROVERBS 4:7

How does one gain wisdom? It comes from experience well handled…or poorly handled. Trials are meant to instruct us in how to live rightly, how to respond with faith and resilience. Every tough spot we're in gives us an opportunity to use—or gain—wisdom.

Father, You tell me to highly prize wisdom, and I do. This present crisis surely has a lesson tucked into it somewhere. Show me, I pray, how to gain the wisdom You have hidden in this hard time.

Lord, open my eyes. Increase my wisdom. Help me learn from this trial so that I can benefit when future trials arise.

The Fear of the Lord

The fear of the LORD is the beginning of wisdom.
PROVERBS 9:10

It's interesting that the fear of the Lord is the beginning of wisdom, and yet we hear so little about it today. We've come to assume that this fear is synonymous with *awe*. But there's far more than awe to rightly fearing the Lord. And when we need a miracle, we're at just the right place in our lives to really "get" the fear of the Lord. We see how powerless we are and how powerful He is. If He won't move on our behalf, our situation is hopeless. But thank God that fearing Him brings wisdom and favor into our lives. As you pray for your miracle, do so as one who is wise—one who fears the Lord your God.

Father God, because I desperately need wisdom, I not only trust in You, but I fear You too. Yes, there is awe in my fear, but there is also the need to lay myself in total surrender at Your feet.

Lord, hear my prayer for wisdom. Teach me to fear You rightly. To love You more perfectly. To learn from You more readily.

All our difficulties are only platforms for the manifestations of His grace, power, and love.
JAMES HUDSON TAYLOR (1832–1905)

THE PARKING PLACE

I will remember the deeds of the LORD;
yes, I will remember your wonders of old.

PSALM 77:11

If God granted your miracle today, would you forget Him tomorrow? There's the old joke about the man who desperately wanted to find a parking place in a crowded city. He prayed, "Lord, if You'll open up a parking place for me, I'll surrender all I have to You—my money, my time, my *life*." Just then, he saw a car pulling out of a parking space ahead of him. He immediately changed his prayer to, "Oh, never mind, God. I found one." No doubt an exaggeration of our response, but let's face it: The need for a miracle keeps us focused on God. For that, we can be grateful. Let your need for God's intervention in your life remain constant, even after the miracle comes.

Lord, if there's one good thing from this crisis, it's that it forces me to rely on You, to call on You, to trust You. When my miracle comes, Father, I will *not* let up in my devotion to You. I will learn from this experience to keep You central in my life. I will live in praise and thankfulness to You for the rest of my days. This is my commitment to You.

A MIRACLE OR GOD'S WILL—
WHICH DO YOU WANT MOST?

Draw near to God, and he will draw near to you.
JAMES 4:8

When we need a miracle, our heart becomes truly exposed. We may wonder what we want most—our miracle or God's perfect will. Make sure the first object of your prayer is seeking God's will, and then pray for the corresponding miracle that both satisfies His will and brings resolution to your crisis.

Lord, though I constantly pray for my miracle, please know that even more than that, I want *You* and Your will as a solution to my situation.

This present need has been drawing me closer to You, and for that I'm grateful. I pray the miracle You send will not only meet my need, but will also be part of Your perfect will. Most of all, I pray I'll always remember that the urgency of this need served the greatest purpose of all—drawing me closer to You.

Claiming the Promise

He has granted to us his precious and very great
promises, so that through them you may become
partakers of the divine nature, having escaped from the
corruption that is in the world because of sinful desire.

2 Peter 1:4

In receiving a miracle, even though it all really depends on God, there is still a part we must play. It's not enough for God to give His promises to us if we won't claim those promises by faith.

I suspect a good many of God's promises to each of us remain unclaimed as we pass through the years. It's a wise Christian who learns to live by God's promises each and every day. Bottom line: God has promised, but you must claim the promise.

God, thank You for Your many precious promises! Thank You that they are meant for *me* (and for any Christian who will live by them). Show me promises in Your Word that are relevant to my present need. Listen to me as I faithfully claim those promises for my desperate situation.

May my faith become anchored in every promise You make to me. May Your faithfulness to me be revealed as every promise comes to pass.

GOD'S DETOUR

*We know that for those who love God all
things work together for good, for those who
are called according to his purpose.*

ROMANS 8:28

We've all been on a road that we expected to bring us to our desired destination, only to find out along the way that there's an unexpected detour we must take. Life is like that. God sees where we are now, and He sees our final destination. But He may also see danger on the interstate that we assume is our safest and most direct route. So, in His faithfulness, He sets up a detour.

At the time, we may resent the detour—it doesn't seem to move us along as fast as we want to go. The sights are not as pretty as they were on the interstate. We don't like being in this unfamiliar territory. But really, don't we know enough yet about the life of faith to prefer God's detour to our own preplanned route? The miracle will come, but sometimes we must endure a detour first.

O Lord, is this present dilemma a detour of Yours? If so, I will pray my way through every mile of the unexpected journey. I will trust that Your detour will bring me safely to my destination.

God, the journey moves more slowly here on this

road of Yours. Hasten the pace when You can. Bring along some sights that I would never have seen on my chosen route. If possible, show me the reason for the detour. But if not, help me simply trust in You mile by mile until the detour folds me back onto the straight highway to my destination.

TRUST AND *OBEY*

If you are willing and obedient,
you shall eat the good of the land.

ISAIAH 1:19

Obedience to God is a key ingredient in the successful Christian life. Many of our trials are of our own making because, in some way, we have launched into an endeavor or relationship that's not sanctioned by God. Even if our trial has not arisen from any disobedience on our part, we still may find our miracle by simply staying on the path of trusting and obeying the Lord. As the old hymn says, "There's no other way."

Father, I'm Your child. And as a child, I want to obey You as I would obey a parent. Help me uncover any act or attitude of disobedience in my life. If there is something I've done that requires restitution, show me that too. Help me be mindful in the days ahead to stay on the path of obedience.

RETURNING THE TOOTHPASTE

You who have made me see
many troubles and calamities
will revive me again;
from the depths of the earth
you will bring me up again.

PSALM 71:20

You know the old saying about how impossible it is to get the toothpaste back into the tube once it's out? That can also describe our difficult times. Perhaps your present situation is due to some adverse circumstance created by your own action or the actions of others. Or maybe it's a diagnosis that can't be put back into the tube.

The good news is that we're not called to retube the toothpaste. It's out now, and God is well aware of it. He is the only one who can take our adversity and restore it or make it turn out unexpectedly to our advantage.

Stop with the toothpaste. It's going to be okay.

Dear God, you see how this situation began. You know whose fault it was or even if it was no one's fault—and the toothpaste just came out of the tube. But now, Lord, I cannot fix things by myself. I need You to bring a miracle into this crazy situation and turn this adversity to my good. I trust You to bring about the right intervention at the right time and in the right way. Father, I wait and watch for You to move.

Immanuel—God with Us

*"Behold, the virgin shall conceive and
bear a son, and they shall call his name
Immanuel" (which means, God with us).*

MATTHEW 1:23

Isn't it great to know we have a God who isn't watching from a distance, but is instead right here with us in our day of trouble?

Rest easy. He is here.

O Lord Immanuel, thank You for Your presence here with me. Thank You that I don't have to summon You from afar or try to pretend You hear my pleas. You simply *do* hear because You're with me. Thank You that I can count on Your presence to comfort me, encourage me, and help me decide how to proceed.

Lord, guide me today. If I must make a decision that bears on my situation, help me make the *right* decision. Show me through circumstances, a word from another person, or simply from a sense of *knowing* this is the right way to go. Be my Immanuel with every choice I must make.

Before You Even Speak

When you pray, do not heap up empty phrases as the
Gentiles do, for they think that they will be heard
for their many words. Do not be like them, for your
Father knows what you need before you ask him.

Matthew 6:7-8

If prayer is not remarkable enough, we serve a God who knows our prayers even before we utter them! How astonishing is that? We can, therefore, have confidence that in His preknowledge of our requests, He is already determining how His will in the matter can accommodate our pleas. Pray, then, with confidence.

Father God, it amazes me that You know my prayers before I even utter them. You read, as it were, my heart. You know what I need even before I know. You find a way, then, to answer with just the right solution that will be in line with Your perfect will.

Lord, read my heart again. Know the needs and cries of my innermost being, for it's there that I worship You.

MEDITATING ON SCRIPTURE

I will meditate on your precepts
and fix my eyes on your ways.
PSALM 119:15

In the Scriptures, we have faith-building encouragement from God. We have great and precious promises, and we also have the story of how God works in the lives of His people. There is so much in God's Word to sustain us. And while reading all those promises and passages of encouragement, it's also important to fully meditate on them.

Find a promise or an encouraging verse, and commit it to memory. But don't stop there. Memorizing is not meditating. Take time to slowly run that memorized verse through your mind. Ponder its meaning. Internalize it. Let it become spiritual food for you.

Here's one of my go-to verses on which I meditate:

You keep him in perfect peace
whose mind is stayed on you,
because he trusts in you.
ISAIAH 26:3

Father, thank You for Your Word. I not only love to read it, but I also treasure it in my heart. I make it my own through meditation. Allow it, Lord, to cleanse my heart, remove my doubts, and calm my fears as

I make it mine. God, speak to me in the depths of my heart through meditating on Scripture. Keep me in perfect peace as I keep my mind stayed on You, not on my circumstances.

Wisdom from Above

*The wisdom from above is first pure, then
peaceable, gentle, open to reason, full of mercy
and good fruits, impartial and sincere.*

James 3:17

It may be that our miracle will come in the form of simply making wise decisions that will bring closure to our trial. God is gracious and a fountain of wisdom, which He longs to share with us. Never fear asking for wisdom to know what to do or how to react. God is eager to give it—and it might be the very miracle you need.

Father, You have invited me to ask You for wisdom, and so I come to You now seeking more than just earthly wisdom—which is often counter to Yours. God, grant me the hunger to ask, the willingness to receive, and the boldness to act on the wisdom You will give me. Lord, if the granting of wisdom is to be the miracle I need, then I ask for it now in Jesus's name.

MIRACLE OR COINCIDENCE?

A scoffer seeks wisdom in vain,
but knowledge is easy for a man of understanding.
PROVERBS 14:6

When your miracle comes, skeptics will tell you it was just a coincidence. Your reply should be, "All I know is that the more I pray, the more coincidences happen!"

Even now, before the miracle appears, scoffers may try to cast doubt in your mind. Don't listen. This miracle is for you. Don't get talked out of it…either before or after it occurs.

Father, Your answers to my prayers may seem like coincidences to others, but to me, they are still miracles from Your hand. And, yes, the more I pray, the more miracles I see.

Lord, never let me take Your movement in my life for granted. I am ever grateful for Your answers to my prayers. May the "coincidences" keep coming!

FORGIVE AND PRAY

Whenever you stand praying, forgive, if you have
anything against anyone, so that your Father also
who is in heaven may forgive you your trespasses.
MARK 11:25

There are only a few places in the Bible where we're given reasons for unanswered prayer. Sin is one reason (1 Peter 3:12). Another is lack of faith (Matthew 13:58). Yet another important reason is unforgiveness. If there is anyone in your hard situation (or outside of it) whom you are not at peace with and must forgive (or be forgiven by), do it now with no hesitation.

God, I try to keep my accounts up to date. I forgive as quickly as an offense comes to mind. Even now, Lord, I pray that if there's someone I need to forgive in order to clear the air, please bring that person to mind. If it's not possible for me to forgive them in person, may I do it with sincerity in my heart.

If there's anyone whom I have offended and must ask for their forgiveness, may You also bring that person to mind. Lord, I want to be free of any root of bitterness due to an unresolved offense.

DOING WHAT MUST BE DONE

*Look carefully then how you walk, not
as unwise but as wise.*

EPHESIANS 5:15

In almost every crisis, there's something that must be done next. If that's the case with your situation, prayerfully plan how to do what must be done, trusting God to lead you in every step. Your willingness to act may hasten the miracle.

Dear Lord, in a hard situation, I'm often paralyzed by the seeming enormity of it all. Help me learn to move forward by giving me courage. Show me exactly what I need to do next on the road to resolving my present trouble. And when there's absolutely nothing I know to do, help me relax and wait on You for instructions on my next step. Let me be neither hasty nor lazy in putting my hand to the plow when I realize what I need to do.

Do All Things in Love

*A new commandment I give to you, that
you love one another: just as I have loved
you, you also are to love one another.*

JOHN 13:34

God is always motivated by His love. He commands us, too, to make love the motive in all we do. What are some ways you can show love to others as you wait for your coming miracle?

God, thank You for Your enduring love. Thank You that my miracle has the word "love" written all over it. As it comes to me, help me manifest genuine love in my own life. Even now, when this present adversity affects my mood and attitude, I pray for love to overcome my natural negativity. Lord, show me practical ways to love others and perhaps hasten a miracle in their life.

GOD'S OWNERSHIP OF YOU

*The Spirit is God's guarantee that he will give
us the inheritance he promised and that he
has purchased us to be his own people. He did
this so we would praise and glorify him.*

EPHESIANS 1:14 NLT

Christians are people who have been purchased by God. God *owns* us. He knew what He was getting when He first loved us and saved us. He knew our issues, our worries, our valleys. He knows the valley you're in right now.

In purchasing you, He has acquired your problems as well—and willingly so. Consider your troubles as belonging not to you, but to God, the One who has the solution and will reveal it in His time. Trust Him.

Father, I'm Yours. You have purchased me, and along with the deal come all my problems, quirks, and missteps. I trust You to handle the issues that are most disturbing to me now. Lord, help me as I once again release these stresses into Your hand.

Bring resolution, Lord. Bring the miracle that represents Your will for my life.

A WAIT OF 32 YEARS

I wait for the LORD, my soul waits,
and in his word I hope;
my soul waits for the Lord
more than watchmen for the morning,
more than watchmen for the morning.

PSALM 130:5-6

I know of a woman whose trial was the callousness of her son, who was showing no interest in Christ. So this mother began to pray for a miracle—the miracle of new birth for her son. She prayed and prayed, and she prayed some more. She prayed for 32 years—and then she died, having seen no change in her wayward son. But did God send the miracle? Were her prayers answered?

Yes! Her son *did* come to know Christ after his mother's death, and he served the Lord for many years. God was faithful, but it was on His timetable, not the praying mother's.

Perhaps your miracle will come tomorrow. Or perhaps it's still years away. Do not give up, even on your dying day. No one could have blamed this man's mother for giving up on her miracle…but she would not be deterred. Neither must you be. Stay the course!

O Lord God, I hope I don't have to wait decades for my miracle! Please grant me an answer soon. Yet not my will, but Yours be done. In Your timing, you will send a miracle. I will stand my ground by believing Your Word and persisting in prayer. I will let nothing stand in my way, not even my death, if it comes to that. Lord, I persist!

A Series of Small Miracles

You are the God who works wonders;
you have made known your might among the peoples.
Psalm 77:14

Sometimes, after we've prayed, we can look back and observe that the large miracle we expected was instead a series of smaller miracles that brought about the same result.

Yes, we love to look for the large, dramatic miracles—and God does send those. Your miracle may be exactly that. Or, it may be that you will one day look back and see that God brought about your resolution through a series of smaller miracles. Either way, you will have reason to rejoice!

God, if it were up to me, I'd just as soon have one large miracle that resolves everything. But I will gladly see the resolution come through a series of small (or even medium!) miracles, if that's Your will.

Lord, if You do send the small miracles, open my eyes to see them. Do not let me overlook what You're doing while my eyes are searching elsewhere for a different answer. To You, a miracle is neither small nor large. It's simply a miracle.

Making a List

When you pray, go into your room and shut the
door and pray to your Father who is in secret. And
your Father who sees in secret will reward you.

MATTHEW 6:6

Many Christians have found that keeping a prayer list is very effective. One way to do this is by writing down your requests on a notepad and creating four columns. In the first two columns, give the request a name and then include the date you began praying for the item. Each day or each prayer time, consult the list and pray for each item, noting any changes in the third column. The final column is where you can add the date when the prayer was answered and the miracle arrived. Such a list can keep you faithful in prayer and build your faith as you record God's answers to your prayers.

Lord, sometimes my prayers seem scattered. Sometimes I even forget to pray for important issues in my life. If a written list will help me focus in prayer, I will start one. As I faithfully pray over my list, I ask You to move in response. Even behind the scenes, when I may think nothing is happening, I pray the items on my list will still be on Your mind. I pray You will bring an answer—Your right answer—to every item I put on my list.

THE ORIGIN OF A MIRACLE

My thoughts are not your thoughts,
neither are your ways my ways, declares the LORD.
For as the heavens are higher than the earth,
so are my ways higher than your ways
and my thoughts than your thoughts.

ISAIAH 55:8-9

Human schemes to fix our problems originate in our earthly minds. That's why they so often fail. But a true miracle can only come from heaven—from the hand of God. Whereas human reasoning belongs to the earthly kingdom, God's reasoning comes from the kingdom of heaven—a huge difference. When we agree to look to God for a miracle, we are also agreeing that a human plan will surely fail. Pray, then, for a miracle that originates in heaven, not on earth.

Dear Lord, I've given up on earthly reasoning, worldly schemes, and human efforts to bring about a solution to my present trouble. Now, Lord, I look to You as the One who originates miracles. You're the One who can solve my problem. You can bring healing. You can restore. So, Lord, bring the miracle straight from heaven's shores. Nothing less will do. Guard me from trusting in "miracles" that are no more than the schemes of man.

PLANTING MIRACULOUS SEEDS IN OTHERS

Let us not grow weary of doing good, for in due season we will reap, if we do not give up.

GALATIANS 6:9

As you go through your valley, others you know are also finding their way along their own hard path. When you pray each day, remember the needs of others. Pray for them in the way you want them to pray for you. Check in with them as often as you can, asking how they're doing. If they have practical needs you can meet (a meal, a drive, or a lengthy conversation over coffee), do so. You will be planting miraculous seeds in the lives of others that will sprout in your own life.

Father, my very real and current need may cause me to gloss over the needs of others near me. I may not hear their unspoken cry or see their private tears. But God, knowing my own need should make me more sensitive to those who are in distress.

Lord, if I'm unaware of the needs of others, bring it to my attention. Sharpen my senses. Remind me of small, practical things I can do to help them. Show me seeds I can plant in the lives of hurting friends that will blossom in my own life as well as theirs.

EXPECT GOD TO HEAL IN HIS PERFECT WAY

After you have suffered a little while, the God of all grace,
who has called you to his eternal glory in Christ, will
himself restore, confirm, strengthen, and establish you.
1 PETER 5:10

Sometimes God is so unpredictable. Faithful, but unpredictable. Right now, as you're praying for your troubling situation, God has sent the answer. It's on its way. It may not be apparent for a while yet, but God has heard. Now your job is to watch Him heal you in His own perfect way.

God, it's hard to keep hoping day after day...but still I wait on You, which makes all the difference. You have heard my cries, collected my tears, and been my comfort on the hardest days. Again, God, I call on You as my Lord to intervene in my situation.

Father, I am helpless. I can do nothing but lean hard on You. Bring healing and restoration soon, in Your own way.

There's Always More

When they had eaten their fill, he told
his disciples, "Gather up the leftover
fragments, that nothing may be lost."
John 6:12

Have you realized that with God, there is never lack, but always *more*? Where we see lack (five loaves and two fish), God sees twelve baskets of leftovers. Where we see our failures, God sees grace to cover our every sin and wrong decision. Where we see a great need in our life, God sees an opportunity to provide for His child.

In your present need, you may see lack, but trust God to multiply the loaves and fish and bring abundance into your situation. He will provide.

Lord, You are the God of plenty in my life. The God of abundance. For my great need, I see only lack. But You see what You have planned. You see restoration. You see the potential for overflowing blessings in my life. You see the end from the beginning.

Lord, give me eyes to see what You see. Help me to perceive what is now invisible to me as You make it reality. Thank You for being the God of *more*.

EXPECTATION

My soul, wait silently for God alone,
for my expectation is from Him.
PSALM 62:5 NKJV

Prayer without expectation is like a wedding without a bride. If we pray, we must expect God to answer. This is not presumption on our part. God invites us to ask Him for our needs. Asking is part of the practice of prayer—along with praise, confession, and listening to God speak to us. God not only invites us to ask, He invites us to *expect*.

So ask away. Then expect away.

Father, You invite me to come to You often with my needs, as I also worship You, confess my sins, and listen to You speak to me. You invite me to expect an answer, looking to You in faith. Lord, as I consider my present dilemma, truly my expectation is from You. Keep my situation ever before Your eyes. Watch over every element of my problem. Devise the perfect resolution and let it manifest soon.

Lord, my expectation *is* from You.

Your Pre-Miracle Miracle

Do not be anxious about anything, but in everything
by prayer and supplication with thanksgiving let
your requests be made known to God. And the peace
of God, which surpasses all understanding, will
guard your hearts and your minds in Christ Jesus.

Philippians 4:6-7

While we pray and wait for God to resolve our problem, we're able to experience an ongoing "pre-miracle" miracle. That miracle is God's peace that passes all understanding, even during *this*, our present trial. Every day while we must wait, God provides comfort, assurance, and encouragement that cannot be explained by human reasoning.

Today, if you have not yet experienced this peace, ask God for it and trust Him to provide. No need to muster up your own version of peace—it simply won't compare with God's supernatural peace.

Father God, I need a peace that passes all understanding as I go through this desert valley. My own attempts to be at peace seem to fail. By Your Holy Spirit, bring that supernatural peace that can sustain me today and every day until my trial is over. Father, give me rest from worry. Provide Your pre-miracle miracle until Your resolution is made apparent. God, thank You for this peace beyond human understanding.

WITHIN EVERY TRIAL

The Helper, the Holy Spirit, whom the Father will send
in my name, he will teach you all things and bring
to your remembrance all that I have said to you.

JOHN 14:26

Within every great trial, there is also a great lesson. But understandably, we're so concerned with the emotional upheaval in our trial, we often can't see the lesson or the possible benefit until much later. That's when we have to take it by faith that God means something good and useful to come out of our troubles. If you can't see it now, may God show you the hidden lesson in this hardship soon.

God, at this point in my trial, it's almost laughable to think there's something good hidden within the situation. I certainly can't see it now. But by faith, I trust that You will bring to light that which is now hidden in my ordeal. By faith, I ask You to maximize that lesson, whatever it is. Lord, may it be worth the pain I'm going through.

Precious Sleep

*I lay down and slept; I woke again, for
the Lord sustained me.*

Psalms 3:5

*It is vain for you to rise up early,
to sit up late,
to eat the bread of sorrows;
for so He gives His beloved sleep.*

Psalm 127:2 nkjv

In the midst of this painful time, while awaiting our miracle, our sleep can be affected in two ways. Either we sleep too much, or we can't seem to sleep well at all. The latter is usually due to worry over our situation. The former is often a way of escaping our pain. In either case, it's right to ask God to help us sleep, to restore us as we lay our head on the pillow at night.

Lord, You know how my trial has affected how I sleep. I see in Your Word that You give Your beloved sleep. God, bring the kind of rest to me that will refresh me. Open the windows of heaven and send in a gentle breeze. May the melodies of heaven be as a lullaby in my ears. May the whispers of comfort from Your Holy Spirit remind me that all will be well. I have nothing to fear and nothing to worry about, for even though I sleep, You never slumber, always at work on my behalf.

Thank You, Lord, for sweet rest.

ABUNDANT ENERGY

Being strengthened with all power, according to his glorious might, for all endurance and patience with joy.

COLOSSIANS 1:11

Severe trials sap our energy. We drag ourselves through the day, listless, purposeless. This is one effect of the depression that can come when we're burdened. At such times, we must do what we can nutritionally to bolster our strength, and we must rely on the Holy Spirit to provide energy to get us through the day.

Father, I need energy to get through this rough patch in my life. Help me take care of myself by reminding me to eat right, exercise, and keep a positive attitude even in the midst of all that's going on. But beyond what I can do, I pray for Your divine energy to infuse me with strength I could never have on my own. I pray for the power to not just make it through the day, but to walk confidently through the maze that's my life right now. Lord, restore my energy.

MUSTARD-SEED FAITH

He put another parable before them, saying, "The
kingdom of heaven is like a grain of mustard seed that
a man took and sowed in his field. It is the smallest
of all seeds, but when it has grown it is larger than
all the garden plants and becomes a tree, so that the
birds of the air come and make nests in its branches."

MATTHEW 13:31-32

We sometimes think we need great faith for God to bring about a great-sized miracle. But it's not the size of the faith that matters; it's the size of the object of our faith. Mustard-seed faith can move mighty mountains if that faith is in a God who can turn geography upside down.

God, my faith may be only the size of a tiny mustard seed, but I place that faith in You, my mighty, powerful, overcoming, miracle-sending God. You, Lord, are my deliverer. You are the promise keeper who assures me that this trial will have the necessary ending resulting from the miracle or series of miracles You will send. God, when I grow weak in faith, remind me to turn my eyes on You and not on myself or my circumstances.

Sanctified Human Reasoning

Do not be conformed to this world, but be
transformed by the renewal of your mind, that
by testing you may discern what is the will of
God, what is good and acceptable and perfect.

Romans 12:2

One often overlooked miracle we can experience during hard times is God bringing the obvious resolution to our minds. In other words, what we must do to resolve our ordeal comes to us in a thought sent by God.

Though sometimes our miracle is God's providential arranging of circumstances to bring about His desired end, other times He simply works through us by leading us step by step to the resolution. We have to be careful, though, to remember that when this happens, we still must acknowledge that it's God's doing, not ours.

God, my own ability to reason is often faulty. I can easily come to wrong conclusions or take missteps based on what I wrongly perceive to be the case. But You, O Lord, can help me think clearly. You can sanctify my human reasoning, giving me insights I would not have on my own. You can show me what to do as I prayerfully think things through.

God, when this happens, help me not allow my emotions to intrude. Instead, may I follow through on Your divine guidance and see the resulting miracle. Lord, guide my thoughts!

Never Early, Never Late

Still the vision awaits its appointed time;
it hastens to the end—it will not lie.
If it seems slow, wait for it;
it will surely come; it will not delay.

Habakkuk 2:3

God has yet to answer a prayer or send a miracle too early or too late. When your miracle arrives—in whatever form it takes—it will be in God's time and in His way. Waiting is hard. But harder still would be an answer to prayer that was untimely.

Lord, though I'm anxious for a resolution to my ordeal, I trust You with the timing of its end and outcome. I pray for and accept by faith Your answer. I determine to have the patience of Job in awaiting Your plan to end this trial. With Your good timing, I pray for peace to be the result of Your intervention—peace and restoration.

THE GREATER WORK

*I have been crucified with Christ. It is no longer
I who live, but Christ who lives in me. And the
life I now live in the flesh I live by faith in the Son
of God, who loved me and gave himself for me.*

GALATIANS 2:20

When we're in the midst of a painful ordeal, we consider God's miracle to be the satisfactory resolving of our crisis. We're so consumed by the emotional toll, we forget that the real miracle God wants to work is *in* us. His plan is always centered on bringing about a greater work inside of us, so that what happens outside of us won't shake us in any way.

Trust God's work in you during this time of crisis. That's His focus. Make it yours too.

Father, I know You mean for this difficult time to help mold my inner life, but some days it's just so hard to see how that can happen. The outward clamor seems to drown out any internal good I might perceive. Yet, even in this, Lord, I do trust You.

I pray You will give me eyes to see the richness You want to produce in me through this hard time. God, I submit as fully as I can to Your work within me.

*We must be careful not to take delays in prayer for
denials... Unanswered petitions...are not blown away
by the wind, they are treasured in the King's archives.*

CHARLES HADDON SPURGEON (1834–1892)

Guard Your Tongue

Whoever guards his mouth preserves his life;
he who opens wide his lips comes to ruin.

PROVERBS 13:3

During times of stress, we need to watch our words. What's in our heart will surely come out of our mouth. Are we speaking hope in Christ? Are we preaching faith in God to ourselves? Or are our tongues reinforcing doubt, thus glorifying the enemy of our souls?

Father, forgive me for foolish talk. When I open my mouth, may my words be statements of praise and affirmations of Your faithfulness to me. When I begin to speak doubt, Lord, put a check in my spirit that will silence such wasted words.

As I spend time in Your Word, may my heart be changed—may it become full of Your wisdom, which then finds its way into my speech. Lord, make my mouth a fountain of praise to You.

Challenge the Enemy

The weapons of our warfare are not of the flesh but have
divine power to destroy strongholds. We destroy arguments
and every lofty opinion raised against the knowledge
of God, and take every thought captive to obey Christ.

2 Corinthians 10:4-5

This present ordeal may, in fact, be a direct hit against you from the enemy of your soul, Satan. God can still redeem the situation and turn it to your good, but in the meantime, you can take a stand against the designs of the enemy through strong prayer. You may need to enter into a season of spiritual warfare where you specifically challenge the enemy and call out his lies. Make no mistake, Satan has a strategy to bring each of us down. We must not be ignorant of his evil devices. Nor must we be ignorant of our mighty weapons against the enemy through the power of Christ.

God, I sense the enemy's hand in my present situation. That won't stop You from providing the miracle that will bring me through, nor will it hinder You working for my good. Even so, I know that now I must take a stand against Satan. I must not be ignorant of his devices.

So God, I call on You as I stand against the enemy. I cast down every evil imagination Satan throws against me. I put on the full armor You provide so that I can withstand his darts. I rejoice in knowing that in

Christ, I have the power to rout the enemy from my life. He has no place in it. Father, I invite You to reveal any areas of my life where I've left myself vulnerable to his attacks. I declare and enforce Your victory in my life over the enemy. Praise You, Father, for my triumph over every satanic attack.

GOD SEES

*Hagar used another name to refer to the LORD, who had
spoken to her. She said, "You are the God who sees me."*

GENESIS 16:13 NLT

Rejected and dejected Hagar had fled from Sarai's
ill treatment. What was she to do? She needed a
miracle.

God sent His angel to her and promised to give her
a son, Ishmael. In response, Hagar referred to God as El
Roi, "the God who sees."

Know that today God has not changed. He is still
your El Roi. He sees what you're going through, and
He cares.

El Roi, You truly are the God who sees. You've seen my
situation from the very beginning. And even now, You
see its end, though it remains hidden from me. Thank
You that because of Your grace, You see with eyes of
compassion, not judgment or rebuke.

Father, I can truly say with Hagar, "You are the
God who sees me."

WHO SHALL SEPARATE US?

I am sure that neither death nor life, nor angels nor
rulers, nor things present nor things to come, nor
powers, nor height nor depth, nor anything else
in all creation, will be able to separate us from
the love of God in Christ Jesus our Lord.

ROMANS 8:38-39

Adversity can make us feel separated from God, even though we know that's not true. Nothing can separate us from the love of God, including "things present."

No matter what your "things present" situation is, no matter the miracle you require, none of it can sever you from God or His love.

Father, I'm in awe of Your overwhelming love that can never depart from me. Nothing in this world can bring an end to it. Your love attends to my prayers. Your love is on my side during times of adversity. Your love gives, never takes.

Lord, may I be so assured of Your care during this hard time that I worry less and love others more.

GOD HAS A PLAN

As for you, you meant evil against me, but God
meant it for good, to bring it about that many
people should be kept alive, as they are today.

GENESIS 50:20

Do you think your situation happened to you randomly, without God's notice? No, God saw this coming and, in fact, devised a strategy from eternity past to use this adversity as part of His plan.

Pray heartily, but trust in God's plan. It's better than yours. Joseph knew this truth, as evidenced in today's verse. Much evil was perpetrated against him, but in the end, he was able to look back and declare that though the intent was evil, God meant it for good. That must be our perspective too.

God, if truth be told, I can devise a plan to end my crisis. In fact, I can picture several miraculous options that I imagine would work out well. However, I'm pretty sure none of my plans are Your plans. You see far differently than me. You see not only my present situation, but also my future, and You know how to fit this ordeal into a perfect plan that resolves the conflict and also brings glory to You.

Lord, I pray Your plan has a miracle attached to it. That's my earnest prayer.

The Safest Place

The name of the LORD is a strong tower;
the righteous man runs into it and is safe.
Proverbs 18:10

During a storm, we want shelter and safety from the blast. And during our present tempest, the safest place on earth is in God's firm grasp. Knowing our sovereign God holds us in His hand, that He controls our situation and its outcome, is really the only thing that can calm our fears.

Come in from the cold. Anchor yourself to your ultimate safe place. Make God your strong tower.

Father, You are my strong tower. You are my safe place during this present turmoil. I run to You for cover. Keep me in Your firm grasp. Resolve my situation soon and in my favor. I trust in Your name, Lord. You are the sovereign director of the events in my life. Every outcome is ordered by You for my good. Bring to pass the end to this present crisis soon, Father.

The "secret of his presence" is a more secure refuge than a
thousand Gibraltars. I do not mean that no trials come.
They may come in abundance, but they cannot penetrate
into the sanctuary of the soul, and we may dwell in
perfect peace even in the midst of life's fiercest storms.
Hannah Whitall Smith (1832–1911)

Coming to Grips

*I have said these things to you, that in me you may
have peace. In the world you will have tribulation.
But take heart; I have overcome the world.*

John 16:33

Sometimes it seems like life is a roller coaster. Up the
steep climb with white knuckles, then down the
other side, laughing all the way. Then perhaps a short
and level ride for a time before we climb again. And it's
during the climbs that we worry and become anxious.
But this is life on planet Earth.

We all must come to grips with both the happy
adventures of life and the heartrending disappoint-
ments. God rejoices with us in the former and comforts and strengthens us during the latter. Coming to
grips with the ups and downs in life teaches us that we
can handle anything if we trust God for the outcome.

Dear Lord, You have confirmed through the words
of Jesus that in this world I will have tribulation—and
I do! But You have also promised peace precisely
because Jesus has overcome the world and its trib-
ulations. In Him, I can have this supernatural peace,
no matter how fiercely the winds of trial blow. Father,
help me stay strong as I come to grips with this roller-
coaster life.

LET THE REDEEMED SAY SO!

Oh give thanks to the LORD, for he is good,
for his steadfast love endures forever!
Let the redeemed of the LORD say so,
whom he has redeemed from trouble.

PSALM 107:1-2

When we're in need of a miracle, we look forward to the day when our troubles are behind us. When that time comes, we must remember to give thanks to our good God for His steadfast love.

We must often call to remembrance His deliverance from our past troubles, and we must say so. We must be ready to give God the glory through the testimony of our lips. Even now, in the midst of our pain, as we still await the miracle, we must give thanks. Our lips must proclaim His redemption.

Father, when this present situation is over, I will give You thanks, even as I do so now. For You're good to me not just when deliverance comes, but even in the midst of my troubles.

Lord, may Your praise be always on my lips. As one of Your redeemed children, may I always be quick to say so—to speak of Your deliverance in my life. May I never wander from Your goodness, and may I never forget Your faithfulness to me.

Take Courage

Have I not commanded you? Be strong and courageous.
Do not be frightened, and do not be dismayed, for
the LORD your God is with you wherever you go.

Joshua 1:9

God commands us to be strong and courageous during our earthly battles and trials. He tells us not to be frightened or dismayed. And why does He tell us this? Because He is with us wherever we go.

If we're going through the fire of affliction, He is there.

If our heart is broken, He is there.

If our finances are gone, He is there.

If the lab results contain bad news, He is there.

No matter our trouble, being courageous is a commandment—and one that we can obey when we know God is with us, no matter what.

Father, as I face my current situation, I feel weak in the knees. Courage seeps out of my heart and mind, only to be replaced by anxiety and fear. Lord, I must remain aware of Your presence with me, wherever I go and whatever my circumstance.

Please, God, allow this trial to help me be the courageous Christian You've called me to be. May I not be frightened, no matter what the coming events in my crisis hold.

Contentment

*I have learned in whatever situation I am to be content.
I know how to be brought low, and I know how to
abound. In any and every circumstance, I have learned
the secret of facing plenty and hunger, abundance and
need. I can do all things through him who strengthens me.*
PHILIPPIANS 4:11-13

Contentment, no matter what our outward circumstances, is something the apostle Paul learned. We can learn it too. We can learn how to stand firm during adversity. We can learn to trust God more fully now than during the days when there are no challenging circumstances. Learn to be content through this trial. Then hold on to that contentment.

Father, adversity in my life tends to undermine my sense of peace. I know I should be content, for You are my provider in every aspect of life. But some days, my current dilemma is overwhelming, and contentment flies out the window. To the best of my ability, Lord, I will learn to be content no matter what state I'm in. Content with Your presence. Content with Your knowledge of my situation. Content with Your miraculous hand in my resolution. Content with Your timing.

Blessed contentment.

LET THIS CUP PASS

*[Jesus] said to them, "My soul is very sorrowful, even
to death; remain here, and watch with me." And
going a little farther he fell on his face and prayed,
saying, "My Father, if it be possible, let this cup pass
from me; nevertheless, not as I will, but as you will."*
MATTHEW 26:38-39

Surely one of our prayers during times of extreme
stress is similar to the Lord Jesus's prayer in the Garden of Gethsemane. Faced with the coming crucifixion,
Jesus prayed that if it were possible, the cup of suffering
might pass from Him. In short, He prayed, "Father, if
there's a Plan B, let's do that." But of course, Jesus followed that plea with, "Nevertheless, not as I will, but
as you will."

It's understandable—even to God—that we, too,
should pray for a painless Plan B...but in so doing, we
must also add, "Nevertheless, not as I will, but as you will."

Father, when I see that Jesus prayed for some other
way—any other way—than the brutal crucifixion He
faced, it gives me consolation for having prayed the
same sort of prayer. Lord, I still pray that if there's a
way out of this ordeal, if there's a workable Plan B
that will accomplish the same thing as this painful
Plan A I'm facing now, then let's do that instead.

Nevertheless, not my will, but Yours be done.

GOD DOES NOT HIDE

He has not despised or abhorred
the affliction of the afflicted,
and he has not hidden his face from him,
but has heard, when he cried to him.

PSALM 22:24

On our darkest days, God may seem to be hidden. But just as the sun is still shining behind the clouds that hide it from our view, so, too, God is still very much with us. He is not hiding. He is here.

God, as I continue my prayers for a miracle, I do so knowing You are very present with me. Though the troubles at hand seem to hide Your face from me, I know that's only my warped perception based on my fears, not my faith.

Father, thank You for never hiding from me. For always being available to hear my cries. For being attentive to my needs. For knowing the exact miracle I require in my life—and for sending it in Your perfect time.

Joy in the Morning

Weeping may tarry for the night,
but joy comes with the morning.

Psalm 30:5

God promises that though our suffering does indeed endure for the night, we can wake up to joy in the morning. When we're understandably focused on our "evening" suffering, it's easy to forget the promise of morning's joys.

Today, take your eyes off the present and instead picture the days ahead when all this is behind you. Picture yourself lavished with joy in the morning. Look forward to it with great anticipation.

O God! The promise of joy in the morning brings me great hope. The night, with its fill of angst and trouble, leaves me desolate. But if I take my eyes off my present suffering, even momentarily, and look ahead to the morning, I feel revived.

Father, I don't know what will happen to bring the morning and its joy, but I do know it will take a miracle. Lord, send the end of my dark night and bring the dawn of a new morning—and joy with it.

FEAR NOT

I, the LORD your God,
hold your right hand;
it is I who say to you, "Fear not,
I am the one who helps you."

ISAIAH 41:13

A crisis in our life usually brings fear. We fear the worst, or perhaps we simply fear the unknown outcome. We may be afraid of change in our life due to our trial. But always, always, always, God stands ready, holding our hand and telling us not to fear.

And why shouldn't we be afraid? Because *He* is the One who helps us.

Father, when fear creeps into my life as a result of this present situation, I take note that You are not only with me in this, but You are at my side, holding my hand.

Lord, I in turn take hold of Your mighty hand and trust in You for the end of this trial. I pray for peace that drives out fear. I pray for Your felt presence during the hardest hours. I pray for Your perfect miracle—Your perfect resolution—for the troubling issues in my life.

FAITH IS YOUR ONLY SOLUTION

*After this many of his disciples turned back and no
longer walked with him. So Jesus said to the twelve, "Do
you want to go away as well?" Simon Peter answered
him, "Lord, to whom shall we go? You have the
words of eternal life, and we have believed, and have
come to know, that you are the Holy One of God."*

JOHN 6:66-69

Some of Jesus's disciples were offended by a "hard
saying" (verse 60). In order to follow Him, Jesus
said they would have to eat His flesh and drink His
blood. As a result, these disciples "no longer walked
with Him" (verse 66).

But Simon Peter knew—as we must know—that,
hard sayings and hard times considered, we have
nowhere else to turn. Jesus alone has the words of eternal life. Faith is our only solution.

Lord, I want to be a true disciple. I cannot be one who
is offended at something You've said in Your Word or
because of some adversity You've allowed into my
life. Father, I have no other place to turn. There is no
other one to whom I *can* turn. You are the Holy One,
and only You have the words of eternal life. Only You
have the miracle I need. You are my only hope. My
only solution.

*Faith never knows where it is being led, but it
loves and knows the One who is leading.*

OSWALD CHAMBERS (1874–1917)

Adversity as an Invitation

Come, everyone who thirsts, come to the waters;
and he who has no money, come, buy and eat!
Come, buy wine and milk without money
and without price...
Incline your ear, and come to me;
hear, that your soul may live...
ISAIAH 55:1,3

God so delights to come into an opened heart that, if need be, He will allow us to be brought to the brink of desperation so that we may earnestly invite Him in. Consider that your present trial—though excruciatingly hard—is an opportunity for a closer walk with God. His invitation stands. If you are thirsty, come to the waters. If you have no money, come, buy, and eat. In the midst of your present sorrow, come to God's banquet.

Father, if this present distress brings me closer to You, it will be worth it. Right now, I just hunger for a resolution. I yearn for a miracle. Lord, as I draw closer to You, hear my cries. See my tears. Send, O Lord, the waters that will quench my thirst. Send the money so I may come, buy, and eat. Bring out the banquet so I might delight myself in Your bounty as I go through this dark valley. Send help, O Lord, so I can tell others of Your miraculous and gracious provision.

WRESTLING

We do not wrestle against flesh and blood, but against the rulers, against the authorities, against the cosmic powers over this present darkness, against the spiritual forces of evil in the heavenly places.

EPHESIANS 6:12

Many of the trials we go through may be inspired by our enemy, Satan. In such cases, our miracle may come about through wrestling against "spiritual forces of evil in the heavenly places." Do not neglect considering this aspect of your trial. You may need to wrestle for your miracle.

Father, I know that some of my trials are simply circumstances playing out in my life. But even then, You use those circumstances to bring about change in me. I know, too, that some trials are satanic attacks for which You're calling me to wrestle against the spiritual forces of evil assailing me.

Lord, I do stand firm against the tactics of the enemy. I wrestle from the position of victory Christ has given me. I take authority over every evil intent waged against me. I resist the efforts of the enemy to bring me down through discouragement or lack of faith. I stand strong against the enemy and in the power of *Your* might.

The Finality of Faith

*Faith is the assurance of things hoped
for, the conviction of things not seen.*
Hebrews 11:1

The real key to victory in our desperate circumstances is to realize the finality of faith. It may have taken us awhile to understand that faith is the beginning and the last point in our journey through Desperation Valley. There simply *is* no other viable option. We must drop all pretense that anything other than God's intervention will do. We are *that* hopeless.

The good news is that this stop in Desperation Valley is our place of rest. We have come to the end of maneuvering, trying to make the unworkable work or attempting to fix the unfixable. Only God can save us now. But this is the best place to be. The finality of faith is having the assurance of things hoped for and the conviction of things not yet seen.

Father, it's so good to know that faith in You is all I have—because faith in You is enough. Faith is my resting place. It's the promise that everything is going to turn out according to Your exact will. It's knowing that You have the right miracle to remedy my situation, and it will come in Your perfect timing.

Yes, Lord, faith is enough. *You* are enough.

A FINAL WORD

Though this book of short prayers now draws to a close, my hope is that you will keep on praying, keep on seeking God whether or not your miracle has come. If it has *not* come, pray on. Have faith—and as has been said several times on these pages, let God provide the miracle of His choice in His time.

If God *has* sent a miracle that resolved your crisis, I want to remind you of an event in Jesus's earthly ministry recorded in Luke.

> On the way to Jerusalem he was passing along between Samaria and Galilee. And as he entered a village, he was met by ten lepers, who stood at a distance and lifted up their voices, saying, "Jesus, Master, have mercy on us." When he saw them he said to them, "Go and show yourselves to the priests." And as they went they were cleansed. Then one of them, when he saw that he was healed, turned back, praising God with a loud voice; and he fell on his face at Jesus' feet, giving him thanks. Now he was a Samaritan. Then Jesus answered, "Were not ten cleansed? Where are the nine? Was no one found to return and give praise to God except this foreigner?" And

> he said to him, "Rise and go your way; your
> faith has made you well" (Luke 17:11-19).

All ten of the lepers were healed. But only one came back and prostrated himself before Jesus, giving thanks. Like him, we must always be thankful to God for His intervention in our lives.

Now you must go forward with a spirit of praise and thanksgiving to your faithful God. You must tell others of how He moved in your life. You must also be there for others in their distress, comforting them with the comfort God has given to you. As Paul reminds us...

> Blessed be the God and Father of our Lord
> Jesus Christ, the Father of mercies and God
> of all comfort, who comforts us in all our
> affliction, so that we may be able to com-
> fort those who are in any affliction, with
> the comfort with which we ourselves are
> comforted by God (2 Corinthians 1:3-4).

One final admonition: If God has helped you through this crisis, surely you must know there will eventually come additional trials and adversities. Such is life on this fallen planet. During the coming hard times, remember to trust in God. Keep this small book handy. Yes, you may need it again.

May God bless you and sustain you through your every trial.

Every Prayer Strengthens Your Marriage

As a husband, you have a unique set of responsibilities weighing on you each day. Your desire is to provide for your wife—and the very best way you can take care of her is by praying for her and your marriage.

Discover biblical direction in this collection of prayers and devotions written for busy husbands like you who need a minute of inspiration.

Dads, Lift Up Your Children in Prayer

Your heart is filled with hopes and dreams for your children, giving you much to pray about each day. These daily prayers and words of encouragement will renew your soul as you intercede in key areas of your child's life, such as learning to forgive, dealing with bullies, accepting discipline, and growing spiritually.

Take a minute out of your day to thank God for your children, and let Him equip you for the challenges of fatherhood with these brief but powerful prayers that will easily fit into your busy schedule.

ABOUT THE AUTHOR

Nick Harrison is the author of more than a dozen books, including several other titles in the One-Minute® Prayers series: *One-Minute Prayers® for Those with Cancer*, *One-Minute Prayers® for Husbands*, and *One-Minute Prayers® for Dads*. His other books include *Magnificent Prayer*, *Power in the Promises*, *His Victorious Indwelling*, and *Promises to Keep: Daily Devotions for Men Seeking Integrity*. Nick and his wife, Beverly—an avid quilter— live in Oregon. Nick's website and blog can be found at nickharrisonbooks.com